M000097225

The advantage to a six-week program is that it f
likely they'll be cramming this program into an alrea
tices, baseball games, and drama club meetings. So a
dating and require less of a time commitment, which means teenagers will be more likely to
stick with it.

But beware: Students might feel rushed during a six-week program. For example, they
might need or want more than one day to discuss their feelings about their parents' divorce
(Week One topic). You might be surprised how easily students will open up and share their
feelings when they're in a safe environment. If you devote two weeks to work through each
chapter, students can take more time to process and discuss what they're feeling and learning.

The advantage of a 12-week program is that it provides ample time for both the discussion and activity portions of each lesson. This Leader's Guide contains group activities for
each week's lesson; however, in a six-week group format, time limitations might not permit
the activity. If you extend it to a 12-week program, you can spend one week in discussion
and the next week devoted to the activity. Spending two weeks on one chapter allows students the opportunity to do the lesson, discuss it in a group format, and take a week to process the information. Students can return the next week, sometimes with a fresh perspective,
and adequately engage in the group activity that's covering the same topic.

But again, beware: A 12-week program might interfere with other activities in the students' schedules. Also, maintaining the students' attention for 12 weeks might be difficult.
Many students jump in and out of activities, and you could lose some of them halfway
through the program. Space is also a concern. Your church might not have enough available
meeting space for your group to meet for 12 weeks.

Consider each point carefully and make the choice that's best for your students' (and
church's) needs.

SUGGESTED SCHEDULE

The following chart clearly explains how to divide each chapter to suit either a six- or 12-
week format; all the work has been done for you.

WEEK #	6-WEEK FORMAT	12-WEEK FORMAT
Week 1	Chapter One	Chapter One Discussion
Week 2	Chapter Two	Chapter One Activity
Week 3	Chapter Three	Chapter Two Discussion
Week 4	Chapter Four	Chapter Two Activity

WEEK #	6-WEEK FORMAT	12-WEEK FORMAT
Week 5	Chapter Five	Chapter Three Discussion
Week 6	Chapter Six	Chapter Three Activity
Week 7		Chapter Four Discussion
Week 8		Chapter Four Activity
Week 9		Chapter Five Discussion
Week 10		Chapter Five Activity
Week 11		Chapter Six Discussion
Week 12		Chapter Six Activity

WHAT YOU'LL FIND IN THIS BOOK

This Leader's Guide contains the same weeklong lessons as the Student Guide. However, the Leader's Guide includes additional information at the end of each lesson to help you conduct the Group Sessions. Another difference between the two guides is that the Scripture references have been written out in the Leader's Guide, while students must use their Bibles to look up the passages for themselves.

Part of the reason we provide you with the material the students are covering on their own is so you can easily and readily add your own questions to the ones we offer in the Group Sessions. Because you know your students best and exactly what aspects of their journaling activities need to be emphasized week to week in group times. We provide the basics, but don't shy away from getting deeper and more specific according to your students' needs. Add to these questions, expand on them, delete ones you don't need. Go to whatever extent is necessary to make this curriculum unique and practical for your group.

At the back of this book we've included a weekly sign-in sheet for students to fill out. This will provide you with the students' contact information, which you'll need should you choose to follow-up with them after the program ends.

You'll also find a sample letter to parents. You might consider sending this letter to your students' parents to explain the program and its goals. If you host a parent information meeting, send this letter about two weeks prior to the information meeting and four weeks prior to the program starting.

Finally, we've included a suggested reading list for both students and parents. You may pass out this information as needed. We believe these books will help both parents and teenagers as they work through the transition of divorce.

DEALING WITH DIVORCE

FINDING DIRECTION WHEN YOUR PARENTS SPLIT UP

ELIZABETH OATES

ZONDERVAN®

ZONDERVAN.com/
AUTHORTRACKER
follow your favorite authors

youth
specialties

youth specialties

Dealing with Divorce Leader's Guide: Finding Direction When Your Parents Split Up
Copyright 2009 by Elizabeth Oates

Youth Specialties resources, 300 S. Pierce St., El Cajon, CA 92020 are published by Zondervan, 5300 Patterson Ave. SE, Grand Rapids, MI 49530.

ISBN 978-0-310-27887-0

Cover design by David Conn
Interior design by Mark Novelli, IMAGO MEDIA

Printed in the United States of America

09 10 11 12 13 14 15 16 17 • 20 19 18 17 16 15 14 13 12 11 10 9 8 7 6 5 4 3 2 1

CONTENTS

To Brandon

INTRODUCTION

Children of divorce reach a crossroads—a point in time when they must choose how they'll live. Will they choose rebellion, self-destruction, and self-satisfaction? Or will they choose the peace and forgiveness found only in Christ Jesus?

Here's what the prophet Jeremiah has to say: "This is what the Lord says: 'Stand at the crossroads and look; ask for the ancient paths, ask where the good way is, and walk in it, and you will find rest for your souls' " (Jeremiah 6:16).

The goal of this curriculum is to help students work through the emotional and spiritual issues of divorce, address their specific needs, and enable them to trust in God's plan for their lives.

WHO WILL BENEFIT FROM THIS CURRICULUM?

Dealing with Divorce is beneficial for middle and high school students, ages 12-18. The curriculum addresses questions, issues, and emotions they might wrestle with whether their parents divorced when they were very young, a year ago, or are currently going through a divorce.

IDEAS FOR FORMING A GROUP

So you want to host a "Dealing with Divorce" group at your church but not sure how to do it? Here are a few guidelines:

Start by getting the word out.
- Mail flyers to your youth group and include visitors. Many students from divorced homes don't have a church home but tag along, visiting their friends' churches. Send letters to all students on your roster, because even if a student comes from an intact home, she might have a friend whose parents are divorced, and she could pass on the information.
- Next, post flyers at your church with the start date and time listed.
- Also, set up an information table a few weeks prior to starting the program. This will allow students and parents to ask questions and look through the curriculum. It'll also give you an

approximate headcount for the group.
- Keep the parents informed. We recommend hosting a parent information meeting about two weeks prior to the program starting. Offer them an outline of the program and let them look through the curriculum. Be open and honest about your intentions for the program—that this is designed to bring about healing and forgiveness for each student. Give parents time to ask questions.

Who should lead a group?
- The number of leaders depends on the size and make-up of your group. If you host a small group of five to 10 students, one leader should suffice. If your group is larger, you'll need more leaders. Plan on one leader for every 10students.
- You also want to consider gender. Guys generally open up more for male leaders, while girls might be more comfortable talking with a female leader. Anticipate the needs of your group and plan accordingly. If you're not sure what your group will look like, plan for one male leader and one female leader. On the first day of your meeting you can decide if you want to stay in one large group for the discussion time, or if your group would benefit more by breaking into gender-specific groups.
- A leader doesn't need to have experience with divorce or be a professional counselor; however, if you can find leaders with such backgrounds, that would certainly help them identify and talk with students. But remember, this curriculum is designed for a small group format, not a counseling session—students will appreciate a leader's compassion more than a professional degree.

Keeping students involved.
- We all know today's students are involved in many activities in addition to school. Our desire is not to cram one more thing into their already overloaded schedules. One way to make this program easier to attend is to schedule it an hour and a half prior to your Sunday night or Wednesday night youth group times. Students generally set this time aside for church anyway, so arriving 90 minutes earlier should be much less disruptive to their schedule.
- Asking students to sign a covenant is also beneficial. The covenant should include their intention to attend each week of the program and also a statement of confidentiality.

PROGRAM DESIGN
The Student Guide includes a six-week Bible study for students to work through independently, followed by a Group Session you'll lead during your youth group or small group meetings. However, as the group leader, you have some flexibility in designing the Group Sessions as either a six- or 12-week program. Advantages exist in both formats.

WEEKLY GOALS

The weekly goals of this curriculum include:

Week One—Road Trip: Identifying Your Feelings About Divorce
- Goal: Help students identify how they feel about and understand God's perspective on divorce.

Week Two—Crimes and Misdemeanors: Exploring Reasons for Divorce
- Goal: Help students better understand why their parents divorced and look at times when God permits divorce.

Week Three—Switching Drivers: Life Changes After Divorce
- Goal: Help students anticipate and deal with any life changes they might experience as a result of their parents' divorce.

Week Four—Driver's Education: How to Effectively Communicate With Your Parents
- Goal: Give students healthy, productive ways to communicate with their parents, stepparents, and stepsiblings.

Week Five—Two Wrongs Don't Make a Right: Choosing Forgiveness After a Divorce
- Goal: Help students find peace through forgiveness and explore the ultimate example of forgiveness: Jesus Christ.

Week Six—The End of the Road: Growing Closer to Christ
- Goal: Show students how they can use the tragedy of divorce to grow closer to Jesus Christ.

GROUP FORMAT

This curriculum works well in a group setting with counselors, teachers, mentors, and other adults leading a small group of students. The leaders needn't be trained, professional counselors.

This curriculum can be administered in either a coed or single-gender group. Determining factors include group size and the students' ages and comfort levels.

Ideally, students will complete the lesson for Week One prior to the first Group Session. This gives them time to explore and process the topic before discussing it in a group setting. If the program is extended to 12 weeks, leaders should encourage the students to review their lesson and spend the week praying over the information before returning for the second week's Group Session covering that particular chapter. This helps ensure the information will still be fresh in their minds.

Each weekly session contains various activities and songs to help foster the discussion. However, these ideas are purely optional. If the group discussion is moving along smoothly, the group leader can opt to continue the discussion and skip the activities. Each student's willingness to share personal experiences varies; therefore the group leader should gauge the need for the activities from week to week.

May God bless your efforts as you work with students arriving at the crossroads of divorce. I pray your students will choose the road that leads to Christ.

ROAD TRIP

Identifying Your Feelings about Divorce

DAY I—ROAD RAGE

Have you ever been driving on a highway when another driver suddenly swerves into your lane, practically cutting off your car's front end? And then that driver has the nerve to honk at you, as if this near-accident were your fault.

Driving, especially in large cities, has become increasingly dangerous over the years. And not just because our country's population has increased—it's also because of people's attitudes on the road.

Have you noticed how drivers begrudgingly allow you to switch lanes? How they run red lights without any hesitation? How they yell at one another for the slightest offenses? Road rage is dangerous and becoming more common in our society. Drivers don't realize their behavior on the road should mirror their behavior when they're outside of their vehicles. Would they act this way in the checkout line at Target? (Well…forget I asked.)

We all experience rage or anger in life. If your parents are divorcing, chances are you feel angry: Angry at your mom, angry at your dad, angry at yourself, angry at God, angry at no one in particular—just angry. Today we'll explore this menace called anger and how we can deal with it in our own lives.

Take a minute to think about situations in the past when your parents have done something to make you angry. Is your dad a workaholic? Does your mom monitor your phone calls? Does your dad miss your football games because he's with his "new family"?

1. Take some time to list (in the space below) any situations or events that have made you angry with your parents.

That was probably easy for you, wasn't it? Holding on to memories that hurt us is often very easy to do. We tend to hold close our memories of betrayal or disappointment.

2. Instead of clutching our anger and never releasing it, what does the apostle Paul say we should do with our anger? Read Ephesians 4:26 and summarize it in your own words.

"'In your anger do not sin': Do not let the sun go down while you are still angry." (Ephesians 4:26)

While our parents might make us angry, we owe them our honesty. Have you ever shared your feelings about your anger with your mom or dad? Have you ever told them about a specific event that really made you angry?

If you've never shared these feelings with your mom or dad, spend some time praying about whether God wants you to approach them. Ask God if your feelings are legitimate, or if you're searching for reasons to be angry with your parents. You might need to spend several days praying about this.

If God tells you to talk about your feelings with your parents, you need to obey God. But there's a specific way to approach them so they'll hear you.

First, schedule a time when you know your mom or dad can sit down with you and really listen. Schedule a meeting in their Blackberry or arrange a lunch or dinner date. They'll appreciate your effort and maturity, and they'll likely respond much more openly than if you were to slyly catch them off-guard.

Second, when you talk with your parents, remember Proverbs 15:1, which states, "A gentle answer turns away wrath, but a harsh word stirs up anger." Be calm. Explain your feelings. Use "I" statements, such as—

- **"I was really angry when** _____ ."

- **"It really hurts my feelings when** _____ ."

Don't use an accusatory tone or "you" statements, such as—

- **"You always** _____ ."

• "You never _____ ."

• "You love _____ more than you love me."

Statements like these will put a wall between you and your parents. The goal of the conversation is to open your lines of communication.

You might be wondering, *What if my parents get angry when I bring up things from the past?* If your parents respond in anger, remember Ecclesiastes 10:4: "If a ruler's anger rises against you, do no leave your post; calmness can lay great offenses to rest." In other words, don't give up and remain calm.

No matter how your parents respond to you, your responsibility is to stand firm in your convictions as calmly as possible. If you feel angry because one parent had an extramarital affair, then you can be honest and tell that parent why this makes you angry. Your mom or dad might be offended by your candor, but you're entitled to express your feelings—as long as you still treat your parents with respect.

Understand anger isn't necessarily wrong or sinful. It's a natural emotion we all—including God—feel. However, our response to this emotion can either be sinful or glorify God.

For the rest of your devotional time, take a look at some other verses associated with anger.

3. Exodus 34:6 states, "The Lord, the Lord, the compassionate and gracious God, slow to anger, abounding in love and faithfulness." What does it mean to be "slow to anger"?

4. How can you become "slow to anger" in your own life?

5. Why does God want us to control our anger? Write down what each verse tells you.

• Proverbs 14:29

> Those who are patient have great understanding, but the quick-tempered display folly. (Proverbs 14:29)

• Proverbs 15:18

> The hot-tempered stir up dissension, but those who are patient calm a quarrel. (Proverbs 15:18)

• James 1:19-20

> My dear brothers and sisters, take note of this: Everyone should be quick to listen, slow to speak and slow to become angry, because our anger does not produce the righteousness that God desires. (James 1:19-20)

6. Instead of negatively responding to our anger, how does God want us to respond? Write down what each verse tells you.

• Galatians 5:22-23

> But the fruit of the Spirit is love, joy, peace, patience, kindness, goodness, faithfulness, gentleness and self-control. (Galatians 5:22-23)

• Ephesians 4:31-32

Get rid of all bitterness, rage and anger, brawling and slander, along with every form of malice. Be kind and compassionate to one another, forgiving each other, just as in Christ God forgave you. (Ephesians 4:31-32)

When someone cuts you off or refuses to let you switch lanes, you have a choice; you reach a crossroads. You either brush off their rudeness, or you get angry and seek revenge.

Life is no exception. You'll experience many trials in which you'll find yourself at a crossroads—a point in time when your attitude and actions will shape your character and your life. Dealing with divorce is a crossroads.

When parents divorce, you have two choices: React in a number of negative ways (which we'll discuss over the next several weeks) or forgive. The easy road is paved with negativity, hurt, and rage. The more difficult road, however, is paved with soul-searching and forgiveness. Navigating your way along the more difficult road requires some help. And that help comes only from Jesus Christ.

Now let's take a few minutes to think about how God feels about divorce.

7. Read the following verses and fill in the blanks.

"I *hate divorce*," says the Lord God of Israel, "and I *hate* it when people *clothe* themselves with *injustice*," says the Lord Almighty. So *be on your guard*, and do not be *unfaithful*. (Malachi 2:16)

For this reason a man will leave his *father and mother* and be united to his *wife*, and the two will become *one flesh*. So they are no longer *two*, but *one*. Therefore what God has *joined* together, let no one *separate*. (Matthew 19:5-6)

Why does God hate divorce? Because God is a God of promises and covenants. God's Word is true and everlasting. When God makes a promise to his children, he follows through. And God expects the same from his children. Marriage is a promise one person makes to another person—and to God. We often think of marriage as a bond between a husband and a wife, but it's really a bond between a husband, a wife, and God. God would never divorce his children; therefore, he doesn't want his children to divorce each other. Divorce is a sin against one's spouse and a sin against God.

God also knows the pain that accompanies divorce. People often believe divorce will solve their problems. Unfortunately, divorce usually just creates new problems. Divorce leaves everyone involved emotionally wounded. God doesn't want to see his children hurt themselves or each other.

"So is God angry at my parents because they divorced?" you might ask.

8. Read the verses below and then write down God's response to his children.

• Psalm 66:20

Praise be to God, who has not rejected my prayer or withheld his love from me! (Psalm 66:20)

• Psalm 86:15

But you, Lord, are a compassionate and gracious God, slow to anger, abounding in love and faithfulness. (Psalm 86:15)

• Luke 15:2

But the Pharisees and the teachers of the law muttered, "This man welcomes sinners and eats with them." (Luke 15:2)

We all sin, whether it's through divorce, cheating on a test, or lying to our parents. And we all need God's love. Fortunately, God loves us despite our sins. Nothing we do can remove God's love from us.

Let's close in a time of prayer.

Dear God,

Thank you for your love and mercy. Thank you for being slow to anger, for loving me when I'm difficult to love, and for being patient with me when I fail you. Please forgive me for the times when I let my anger control my thoughts, words, and actions. I pray you'll make it clear whether you want me to approach my mom or dad about things that have made me angry in the past. Help me to clearly understand your will and obey. Help me to control my anger so my words and actions are a reflection of you. Amen.

DAY 2—CAUTION WHEN WET

Sadness is another emotion you might feel as a result of your parents' divorce. It's a loss in your life, in the same way that it's a loss if you get cut from the basketball team, your best friend moves to another city, or your favorite aunt passes away. They're all losses, even though we experience different levels of grief about the different losses.

Divorce causes us to feel sad for many reasons:

- We want our parents to get back together.
- We hate all the fighting.
- We believe the divorce is our fault.
- We want things to go back to the way they used to be.
- We feel replaced when one parent finds a "new family."

1. All of these thoughts lead to sadness. What are some other things about divorce that make you sad?

But knowing we feel sad doesn't take away the sadness. We must also express our feelings. In the Old Testament, the Israelites expressed their sadness in several ways.

2. Look up the following verses and describe their reactions to grief:

- 2 Samuel 1:11-12

Then David and all the men with him took hold of their clothes and tore them. They mourned and wept and fasted till evening for Saul and his son Jonathan, and for the army of the Lord and the house of Israel, because they had fallen by the sword. (2 Samuel 1:11-12)

• 2 Samuel 12:15-17

> After Nathan had gone home, the Lord struck the child that Uriah's wife had borne to David, and he became ill. David pleaded with God for the child. He fasted and spent the nights lying in sackcloth on the ground. The elders of his household stood beside him to get him up from the ground, but he refused, and he would not eat any food with them. (2 Samuel 12:15-17)

• Jeremiah 48:37

> Every head is shaved and every beard cut off; every hand is slashed and every waist is covered with sackcloth. (Jeremiah 48:37)

Wow! Those Israelites weren't afraid to express their feelings. In our Western society, however, we're often taught to mask our feelings, to just "get over it." We're often even denied the right to be sad.

3. How do you express your sadness?

If you haven't yet found some constructive, healthy ways to deal with your feelings, here are some ideas:

• **Pray.** Let God know about your feelings. Confess everything to him. God already knows what's on your mind, so why not verbalize it to him? Second Corinthians 1:3 says, "Praise be to the God and Father of our Lord Jesus Christ, the Father of compassion and the God of all comfort."

• **Write in a journal.** Journaling your thoughts and feelings is something both guys and girls can do. Some guys are wary of doing this, but rest assured there are many men all over the world who are discovering the power of writing down their thoughts and emotions. Don't be afraid to put on paper what's in your head and heart. This process will help you sort through your thoughts and feelings and make sense of your emotions.

• **Talk to a trusted friend or relative.** This can seem scary because you're revealing yourself to someone. You're becoming vulnerable—not a comfortable act for most people. However, finding one trustworthy person will free you from carrying these burdens by yourself.

Expressing sadness or hurt can be especially difficult for young men. Guys, you're often taught that "boys don't cry," right? Well, that philosophy is wrong. The Bible tells us that men from the beginning of time have cried—even torn their clothes, shaved their heads, and fasted. And all as means of expressing their despair.

Our society also tells us to "pull ourselves up by the bootstraps." Our culture deems grieving as inappropriate and a waste of time. However, ignoring your feelings won't cause them to magically disappear. You must deal with your feelings.

One reason you should deal with your sadness is because sadness can lead to depression—a serious illness that affects one in 10 teenagers in the United States.[1] That's 2.2 million people your age—and just in America!

Do you think you might be depressed? Do you know someone who's depressed? Here are some signs that depression might be affecting you[2]:

• **Poor concentration**—Does your mind wander during class, when you study, or in the middle of a conversation with someone?

• **Headaches, stomachaches, or other ailments**—Do you suddenly feel more run down or notice more frequent headaches?

• **Changes in sleeping behavior**—Do you stay up all night playing video games? Do you sleep all day, sometimes even missing school because you can't or don't want to get out of bed?

• **Changes in eating behavior**—Has your appetite decreased? Or is the opposite true—do you turn to food for comfort, sometimes eating when you aren't even hungry?

• **Feelings of guilt, hopelessness, worthlessness, or helplessness**

• **Fatigue**

• **Loss of interest in favorite activities or hobbies**

• **Thoughts of death or suicide**

If you recognize any of these behaviors in yourself or in a friend, please take action:

• **Pray!** The prophet Jeremiah says, "You who are my Comforter in sorrow, my heart is faint within me" (Jeremiah 8:18). Do you feel like this sometimes? Don't give up! God reassures us, "The Lord is close to the brokenhearted and saves those who are crushed in spirit" (Psalm 34:18).

• **Talk to a trusted parent, friend, teacher, or relative.** Let this person know which of these feelings and behaviors you're experiencing.

Sadness can lead to depression, and depression can sometimes lead to suicide. In the year 2000, approximately 3 million adolescents, ages 12 to 17, either thought seriously about suicide or attempted suicide.[3] Don't let your sadness spin out of control. Please seek help so you can overcome your feelings and begin to experience the abundant blessings God has planned for you.

God's people have often felt overwhelmed by their sadness and grief. But God promises us he'll "turn their mourning into gladness" and "give them comfort and joy instead of sorrow" (Jeremiah 31:13).

Use the rest of your quiet time today to confess your feelings to God. If you're sad, tell him why you feel this way. Ask God to heal your broken heart. Trust that God has blessings prepared for you.

DAY 3—ABANDONED VEHICLE

When I was about two years old, my mom and dad divorced. Without going into details, I can say my dad was an unhealthy person physically, emotionally, mentally, and spiritually. He faded in and out of our lives for the next seven years, which created a distant and confusing father-daughter relationship. Finally, when I was about eight years old, my mom, brother, and I moved across the country.

I don't know what separated my dad and me more: The vast geographical distance or the unsettling emotional distance. For whatever reason, my dad stopped calling, writing, and sending birthday cards. Various relatives would give us the latest news of his whereabouts, jobs, and so on. But eventually we stopped asking, and they stopped volunteering the information. By the time I turned 10 years old, my dad's absence in my life was official.

I really don't remember missing my dad or wishing he played a stronger role in my life because our relationship had always been inconsistent and uncomfortable. His absence had always been more reliable than his presence.

Once, when I was in college, a good friend of mine asked me if my dad was dead. I stood there shocked…confused…speechless.

"Of course he's not dead. Why would you think that?" I asked.

"Because you never talk about him," my friend said.

Hmmm… I'd never realized how little I thought or talked about my dad. I'd made a habit of ignoring the topic altogether, pretending everything was "normal" and convincing myself that most children of divorce don't have a relationship with one of their parents.

While some fathers abandon their children after divorce, many other dads continue to play an important role in their children's lives. Let's not forget those dads who sacrifice time, money, and energy to spend time with their children.

Don't worry: We aren't just picking on the dads. Unfortunately, some moms can't handle the stress of the divorce or the responsibility of raising children on their own and jump ship themselves. Will Smith's film *The Pursuit of Happyness* (Columbia Pictures, 2006) portrays a father trying to create a better life for himself and his son after his wife abandons them both. This movie, based on the true story of Chris Gardner, shows a father committed to his child. In an interview with Oprah Winfrey, Chris said his greatest accomplishment wasn't getting a better job or providing more material things for his son—his greatest accomplishment in life was breaking the cycle of child abandonment in his family.[4]

Parents abandon their children in many ways, including physically, emotionally, mentally, spiritually, and financially. Has your mom or dad abandoned your family? Does she show up only at her convenience? Does he refuse to pay child support or help with financial obligations like school, extracurricular activities, and clothes?

1. Do you feel deserted by a parent? If so, how does that make you feel? Look at the choices below and check all the feelings that apply to you:

- ❑ I feel worthless.
- ❑ I feel unloved and unlovable.
- ❑ I feel like I'm not important.
- ❑ I don't feel good-looking enough, smart enough, athletic enough,
  _____ enough.

2. How has your parent's absence affected you?

- ❑ I struggle with fear.
- ❑ I struggle with self-worth (accepting myself as I am).
- ❑ I struggle with self-esteem (realizing my positive qualities and all that I have to offer).

❑ I'm afraid to depend on other people.
❑ I avoid making close friendships and opening up to people about my feelings.
❑ I'm angry and bitter.
❑ I'm sad most of the time.
❑ I worry about the future.
❑ I'm indifferent.
❑ I'm happy my parents have found happiness, even if it's a result of their divorce.

People often ask me if I'm angry with my father for abandoning my brother and me. Honestly, I harbor no bitterness, anger, or blame. I know there's more involved in my situation than one man's inability to be a father. I believe God has protected me in many different stages and areas of my life, and the absence of my father is a crucial example of God's protection.

As I said, my father was unhealthy in many ways. While I don't remember much about my dad, the memories I carry with me aren't positive. I truly believe God used my father's absence to protect me from further physical, emotional, and mental harm.

But many of you may not feel so blessed by your parent's absence. If you struggle with feelings of abandonment, please know that God cares for you. Throughout the Bible, God addresses the issue of those who've been abandoned by their fathers. Take some time right now to read the following passages and answer the questions.

3. According to the verses below, what's God's promise to abandoned children?

• Psalm 10:17-18

You, Lord, hear the desire of the afflicted; you encourage them, and you listen to their cry, defending the fatherless and the oppressed, so that mere earthly mortals will never again strike terror. (Psalm 10:17-18)

• Psalm 27:10

Though my father and mother forsake me, the Lord will receive me. (Psalm 27:10)

• John 14:18

"I will not leave you as orphans; I will come to you." (John 14:18)

Even when we feel abandoned and forgotten by our earthly parents, God will never leave us. God loves us and cares for our every need. Psalm 68:5 promises, "A father to the fatherless, a defender of widows, is God in his holy dwelling."

Let's close in prayer today.

Dear God,

Thank you for promising me you'll never leave me. Thank you for assuring me you'll always provide for me. While I feel abandoned by _____, I know you'll never leave me. Help me to forgive _____. I pray I'll take comfort in knowing you'll never leave me. Amen.

DAY 4—STUCK ON THE SIDE OF THE ROAD

My parents divorced when I was very young, and my mom remarried when I was in middle school. When I was about 13 years old, my brother and I drove to our family's lake house. My mom and stepdad had driven down earlier in the day, so my brother and I left town after school that Friday afternoon. The sun set as we drove, and eventually we were traveling down the highway in darkness. Suddenly we heard a pop. The entire Jeep shook. We pulled over to the side of the road as cars zipped past us, and we discovered a nail stuck in the back right tire.

I shouldn't have worried; my brother is very capable in these sorts of situations. But I still bit my lip to keep from crying. Believe it or not, this event occurred back in the day before everyone had cell phones, text messaging, and rollover minutes. Yes, there was such a time. (And I'm not even that old.) We were stuck on the side of the highway, in the dark, with no way to call anyone, and no one to rescue us.

My brother immediately took action. He kept a spare tire in the back of the Jeep, so he started changing the tire. My only responsibility was to hold the flashlight. But I was so nervous about the hundreds of cars speeding past us that I couldn't concentrate. Then I stepped into a huge ant hill, causing ants to scurry all over us. Needless to say, my brother wasn't too happy with me.

He eventually got the tire changed and we got back in the car. But I was still worried. What if we got another flat tire? What if the car broke down altogether? What if no one ever heard from us again? I sat in fear and silence during the rest of the drive until we finally reached the lake house.

What do you think of when you hear the word *fear*? Do you think of that scary slasher movie you watched at your best friend's house? Or of telling your parents you got a D on your report card? If your parents divorce, fear becomes something much more paralyzing.

The term *worry*, as you know, involves an *anticipation* of danger—you spend time thinking about something that hasn't yet occurred and may not occur. Worry also evokes a sense of anxious concern. Our thoughts are preoccupied, and this preoccupation causes some anxiety. I was definitely worried, anxious, concerned, and preoccupied the night I stood on the side of the road after our Jeep got a flat a tire.

1. When you think of your parents' divorce, do you feel anxious, concerned, or afraid? Use the space below to describe your feelings of fear or worry.

Worry involves spending time, energy, and emotions thinking about things that haven't even occurred. In the wake of divorce, we often worry about—

- **Money**—Will my mom be able to find a job that can support us? Will one parent have to pay child support?

- **Relationships**—Will Mom keep in touch with me when I go live with Dad? Will Dad still come to my soccer games? Will my parents remarry?

- **Moving**—Will we have to move to a different house? A new city?

2. Do any of these things worry you? List the things you're afraid of or worry about concerning your parents' divorce.

Now read Matthew 6:25-34.

> "Therefore I tell you, do not worry about your life, what you will eat or drink; or about your body, what you will wear. Is not life more important than food, and the body more important than clothes? Look at the birds of the air; they do not sow or reap or store away in barns, and yet your heavenly Father feeds them. Are you not much more valuable than they? Can any one of you by worrying add a single hour to your life?
>
> And why do you worry about clothes? See how the flowers of the field grow. They do not labor or spin. Yet I tell you that not even Solomon in all his splendor was dressed like one of these. If that is how God clothes the grass of the field, which is here today and tomorrow is thrown into the fire, will he not much more clothe you—you of little faith? So do not worry, saying, 'What shall we eat?' or 'What shall we drink?' or 'What shall we wear?' For the pagans run after all these things, and your heavenly Father knows that you need them. But seek first his kingdom and his righteousness, and all these things will be given to you as well. Therefore do not worry about tomorrow, for tomorrow will worry about itself. Each day has enough trouble of its own." (Matthew 6:25-34)

This text focuses on the people's preoccupation with accumulating material possessions, but the application stretches far beyond our material needs. While we do worry about material things, we also worry about things such as making the basketball team, getting the lead in the school play, passing our driver's test, meeting our mom's new boyfriend, taking care of our dad, and many other situations.

Let's focus on two key verses from this passage. In Matthew 6:32-33 Jesus tells the people, "and your heavenly Father knows that you need them. But seek first his kingdom and his righteousness, and all these things will be given to you as well."

First, Jesus assures the people that God already knows their needs. Note that Jesus says "needs," not "wants." We need food, shelter, clothing, love, and safety. We don't need the newest Xbox, a trendy pair of jeans, or a week at summer camp. Those are all "wants." Sure, they might have been a part of your life when your parents were married, but economic changes often accompany divorce.

Next, Jesus tells the people that God will give them all they need "from day to day." As a self-professed type-A personality, I'm naturally bent toward impatience. I often use the microwave because I don't want to wait more than 10 minutes for my food to cook. I fast-forward through commercials on my TIVO because I don't have the patience or interest to watch them.

Obviously I'm not going to win the "most patient" award anytime soon. God, however, is patient beyond compare. God doesn't promise he'll fulfill our needs all at once, a month in advance, or with ample notice. No, God promises he'll take care of us "from day to day."

3. Why would God choose to provide for us in this way?

God teaches us many things by giving us just what we need right when we need it.

First of all, God teaches us patience (my personal favorite). We receive God's blessings and must wait for more without feelings of entitlement. Second, God also teaches us humility as we realize he alone can provide for our needs. While God loves us, he doesn't need us to accomplish his will. That's a big shock to such an ego-centered culture like ours. Finally, God teaches us thankfulness. When we spend time living without certain things, we experience a greater appreciation once we receive them.

So what does it mean to live for God? It means to devote our thoughts and actions to eternally significant things.

4. List some eternally significant things in which we should invest our time and energy.

While this answer will differ for everyone, all answers have a common bond. Things of eternal significance include that which is important to Jesus Christ. What's important to Jesus Christ? Worshiping God and loving people. If your answer involves these two things, rest assured you understand what's eternally significant.

If you have any worries or fears, confess those to God in the following space. Ask God to forgive you for not trusting him to fulfill your needs. Ask God to help you trust him and rely on him in the future.

DAY 5—IT WAS MY FAULT

When my mom remarried, we relocated from a big city to a small town. Moving there proved more difficult than I expected. Cliques ruled the school. Our own *Mean Girls* entourage made me their target—I guess it was my initiation as the new girl. But after a couple of years, I adjusted and actually enjoyed my new life in a small town.

During my high school years, just as I was feeling more comfortable at school, my mom and stepdad divorced. My stepdad and I had always clashed, although most times I didn't even know why he was mad at me. He and my mom fought a lot, and many times the fights centered on me. But when they divorced, he revealed the deep-seated truth that had driven a wedge between us all those years.

I was of no use to him. He had two older daughters from a previous marriage and didn't need another one. He was jealous of the time I spent with my mom and the attention I received from her. I'd never understood. It didn't make sense. Until then.

At that moment I stood at a crossroads in life. I could respond in two ways: Internalize his words, carry around the (false) guilt of breaking up a marriage, and believe I was no use to anyone by quitting the tennis team and cheerleading and letting my grades drop.

Or I could take the other path and believe I was valuable, important, and worthy of love.

You see, while my stepdad blamed me for many things, I knew the truth: Whatever his issues were with me, they were *his* issues. I refused to let him make me feel guilty or accept responsibility for the divorce. I remained involved in my extracurricular activities and maintained good grades because I knew I was of great worth in God's eyes, and I refused to believe such destructive lies.

1. Think about your own parents' divorce for a minute. Do you feel guilty for any reason? If so, write down your thoughts and feelings.

If you feel guilty—as if you contributed to your parents divorce somehow—examine why you feel this way. Then talk to a trusted friend or adult. That person can help you sort through your feelings. Chances are good that you're not responsible for your parents' troubles.

In fact, kids are almost *never* responsible for their parents' divorce. So why would parents believe the kids were at least partly to blame? Well, because kids need a lot from their parents: Time, money, energy, and attention—just to name a few.

But what many parents forget is that children are a privilege, not a burden. You are valuable, special, and worthy of love.

While kids aren't responsible for their parents' divorce, sometimes they do contribute to stress in the marriage. Sometimes kids purposefully try to sabotage their parents' relationship, especially in stepfamilies. Think about your relationship with your own parents. Have you ever manipulated them to get what you want? Have you lied to them? Have you used one parent against the other? While these things may not have broken up the marriage, they do create stress in the family.

2. If you recognize these or any other behaviors, confess them to God. Psalm 51:9-10 says, "Hide your face from my sins and blot out all my iniquity. Create in me a pure heart, O God, and renew a steadfast spirit within me." Search your heart and ask God for forgiveness.

We need to confess our feelings because if we feel guilty, then we're unable to fully receive God's love. Confession is the foundation of salvation. Guilt creates a barrier between us and God. When we feel guilty, we must confess to God the things we've done wrong; and if you're not already a Christian, you can tell God that you want a better way to live and ask Jesus to come into your heart to be your Lord and Savior.

When Jesus becomes our Lord, this means he becomes our boss. Jesus tells us what to do and how to do it. If we have a question about how we should do something, then we can go to him. If we have trouble with a friend, a family member, or a general situation, we take our concerns to Jesus.

He's also our Savior. Jesus helps us navigate through life so we might live it more abundantly. Without Jesus we can never experience true joy or peace.

Having Jesus as our Savior also means only he can rescue us from eternal death. Have you ever thought about what would happen to you if you died tomorrow? It's a scary thought for some people because they don't know their fate. If you know Jesus as your personal Lord and Savior, you can be confident you'll be in heaven with Jesus.

"But I'm a good person," you might say. "I don't lie, drink, or steal. I make good grades. I'm a pretty good kid. Surely God will let me into heaven."

3. To see what Scripture says, look up the following verses and copy them into the spaces provided.

• Romans 3:23

For all have sinned and fall short of the glory of God. (Romans 3:23)

• Ephesians 2:8-9

For it is by grace you have been saved, through faith—and this is not from yourselves, it is the gift of God—not by works, so that no one can boast. (Ephesians 2:8-9)

Every time we gossip, we turn away from God. Every time we watch something on TV that's not glorifying to God, we turn away from God. Every time we drink at a party, we turn away from God.

But despite all of our mistakes, we can always turn back toward God. In Romans the apostle Paul assures us, "If you declare with your mouth, 'Jesus is Lord,' and believe in your heart that God raised him from the dead, you will be saved" (Romans 10:9).

Take the time right now to examine your own life. Do you feel consumed by guilt? Are you overwhelmed with life? Have you ever asked Jesus to be your personal Lord and Savior? Confess your sins to God.

If you're a Christian, ask God to give you the strength and wisdom you need to be a positive witness for him. If you aren't a Christian, then ask God to cleanse you of your sins, to reign in your heart, and to be your personal Lord and Savior.

If you just prayed this prayer for the first time, please talk to someone about it—a trusted friend or family member, a counselor, or your youth pastor. Tell someone about your decision to accept Christ and ask that person to pray for you during this exciting time in your life.

GROUP SESSION
WEEK ONE—ROAD TRIP
Identifying Your Feelings about Divorce

GOAL
This week you'll allow the students to discuss their feelings about their parents' divorce. You'll also look at God's thoughts and feelings about divorce and commitment.

SUGGESTED ICEBREAKER
You'll need:
- A copy of "Father of Mine" (*So Much for the Afterglow*, 1997)
- A CD player

Let the students listen to "Father of Mine" by Everclear (*So Much for the Afterglow*, 1997). You might want to find the lyrics online and print copies of them so the students can read the words while they listen to the song.

After the song ends, discuss the following questions:

1. What emotions do you think the singer has experienced as a result of his parents' divorce?

2. The singer feels abandoned by his dad after the divorce. Can you identify with his feelings? Why or why not?

3. What other feelings do you experience as a result of your parents' divorce?

GROUP DISCUSSION
Continue exploring students' thoughts and feelings about their parents' divorce by discussing the questions below. This discussion will also help them reflect on Week One's Bible study, which they've already worked through independently.

If time allows, ask the students to look up some or all of the following verses and answer the questions:

Anger

• Do you feel angry about your parents' divorce? Why or why not?

• How do you express your anger?

• How does God want us to express our anger according to Ephesians 4:26?

> "In your anger do not sin: Do not let the sun go down while you are still angry. (Ephesians 4:26)

• According to what you read this past week, how does God feel about divorce?

• What are some constructive ways we can express our anger?

Sadness/Depression

• Do you feel sad about your parents' divorce? Why or why not?

• How do you cope with your sadness?

• How can we express our sadness in healthy ways?

• Explain the difference between sadness and depression. What are some signs of depression? What should you do if you feel depressed?

• According to 2 Corinthians 1:3, why does God want us to praise him when we're sad?

> Praise be to the God and Father of our Lord Jesus Christ, the Father of compassion and the God of all comfort. (2 Corinthians 1:3)

. . . .

If your group meets for 12 weeks, wrap up the session after discussing sadness/depression and close simply in prayer and be open to any questions from your students. (Anger and sadness are the two most common feelings students associate with divorce, so they'll be most willing to talk about these emotions.) Discuss the remaining feelings slated for this session during Week Two's session.

As an icebreaker for Week Two, ask how they're feeling this week in general. Has anything happened in the past week that has stirred up strong emotions? Use this as a time to allow students to open up, encourage one another, and move to a deeper, more personal level of sharing. (And use the Closing Activity listed here as the Closing Activity for Week Two.)

Remind students to read over their Week One (Chapter One) homework before the next meeting. Also, encourage them to spend the week praying about their feelings. If they have negative feelings, encourage them to talk to a trusted friend, adult, their parents—or you. They should also seek God's help in working through these feelings.

....

Abandonment

• Do you feel abandoned by one or both of your parents? If so, why?

• Read Psalm 68:5. How can God be "a father to the fatherless"?

A father to the fatherless, a defender of widows, is God in his holy dwelling. (Psalm 68:5)

Fear/Worry

• What things worry you regarding your parents' divorce?

• How does God want us to respond to our fears and worries? (Matthew 6:33-35)

But seek first his kingdom and his righteousness, and all these things will be given to you as well. Therefore do not worry about tomorrow, for tomorrow will worry about itself. Each day has enough trouble of its own. (Matthew 6:33-35)

• Why does God want us not to worry?

Then Jesus said to his disciples: "Therefore I tell you, do not worry about your life, what you will eat; or about your body, what you will wear. Life is more than food, and the body more than clothes." (Luke 12:22-23)

Guilt

• According to Ezekiel 18:19-21, what's God's promise to us regarding our sins?

"Yet you ask, 'Why does the son not share the guilt of his father?' Since the son has done what is just and right and has been careful to keep all my decrees, he will surely live. The one who sins is the one who will die. The child will not share the guilt of the parent, nor will the parent share the guilt of the child. The righteousness of the righteous will be credited to them, and the wickedness of the wicked will be charged against them. But if the wicked turn away from all the sins they have committed and keep all my decrees and do what is just and right, they will surely live; they will not die." (Ezekiel 18:19-21)

Other Feelings Students Might Experience

- Relief
- Desire for a stable home
- Responsibility for, or protective of, one parent
- Blame toward one parent

Let the Students Know

- Their feelings will change throughout the divorce and afterward.
- They should have someone in their lives with whom they can talk about their feelings: A friend, teacher, coach, a friend's parents, an aunt or uncle, and so on.
- They should find ways to communicate with their parents about their feelings.

CLOSING ACTIVITY

Ask the students to cut and paste magazine clippings to make a collage expressing their feelings about divorce. Students may work either in groups or individually, based on group size and the amount of materials on hand.

Close this session with a group prayer, asking God to help everyone work through their feelings to bring about healing.

YOU'LL NEED—
- Magazines (include magazines that appeal to both genders)
- Scissors
- Markers
- Glue
- Sheets of poster board or construction paper

CRIMES AND MISDEMEANORS

Exploring Reasons for Divorce

*Sometimes trying to understand **why** our parents divorced is the most confusing part of dealing with it. This week we'll discuss the many reasons why parents divorce. We'll also examine what God says about divorce.*

DAY 1—EXCEEDING CAPACITY

During my sophomore year in high school, I was the first one of my friends to get my driver's license. One rule my mom gave me was that only three other people could ride in the car with me. This was a problem, however, because I had more than three friends. Our school offered off-campus lunch, and my friends all wanted a ride to Taco Bell or McDonald's on a daily basis. I crammed up to six girls in my four-door Honda Accord, and while we had fun, we weren't safe. The car was designed to hold a maximum of five passengers; my little Honda toted around seven!

The same rule applies to marriage—there's room for only two people. A person commits adultery when they bring a third person into the relationship. Adultery seems exciting and thrilling to some people, but it's often lethal to a marriage. Adultery betrays trust and honor. It creates a wound so deep that sometimes people cannot repair the damage.

Adultery, unfortunately, has existed since the beginning of recorded time. And it's so destructive that God included it in the Ten Commandments (see Exodus 20:14, Matthew 19:9, and Mark 10:19).

"You shall not commit adultery." (Exodus 20:14)

"I tell you that anyone who divorces his wife, except for marital immorality, and marries another woman commits adultery." (Matthew 19:9)

"You know the commandments: 'You shall not murder, you shall not commit adultery, you shall not steal, you shall not give false testimony, you shall not defraud, honor your father and mother.'" (Mark 10:19)

Much debate swirls around what exactly constitutes adultery. The textbook definition is sexual intercourse outside marriage; but others believe adultery doesn't equal sex only—that it can also mean everything from kissing to a romantic conversation with, or emotional attachment to, someone outside the marriage.

1. What does God consider to be adultery according to Matthew 5:27-28?

> You have heard that it was said, "You shall not commit adultery." But I tell you that anyone who looks at a woman lustfully has already committed adultery with her in his heart. (Matthew 5:27-28)

2. In Proverbs 6:32 God says those who commit adultery are fools. Why?

> But a man who commits adultery has no sense; whoever does so destroys himself. (Proverbs 6:32)

Have you ever heard this saying?

> *Sin will take you farther than you wanted to go, cost you more than you wanted to pay, and keep you longer than you wanted to stay.*

I love that quote because it's so *true*! Adultery usually begins as "innocent flirtation," but it lures people to form a deeper relationship—the kind of relationship that should exist only between a husband and wife. What may begin as a few friendly lunches can eventually evolve into a drawn-out, time-consuming relationship. And in the end, adultery costs people their families, friends…everything.

If one or both of your parents have committed adultery, our purpose here is not to condemn them, but to help you understand why adultery contributed to the divorce. God created the marriage covenant as something sacred and binding, yet adultery can destroy that bond. Mark 10:9 is read at many weddings, including my own.

3. Please summarize Mark 10:9 in your own words. "Therefore what God has joined together, let no one separate."

The goal is not to place blame on either of your parents, but for you to understand the consequences of adultery so one day, if you're married, you'll protect yourself against this destructive sin. You're standing at a crossroads in life—a time to develop your beliefs and character. The goal is to take all of your life experiences, including your parents' divorce, and learn from them. Learn from the mistakes as well as the blessings.

Read John 8:1-11 and answer these questions:

> But Jesus went to the Mount of Olives.
>
> At dawn he appeared again in the temple courts, where all the people gathered around him, and he sat down to teach them. The teachers of the law and the Pharisees brought in a woman caught in adultery. They made her stand before the group and said to Jesus, "Teacher, this woman was caught in the act of adultery. In the Law Moses commanded us to stone such women. Now what do you say?" They were using this question as a trap, in order to have a basis for accusing him.
>
> But Jesus bent down and started to write on the ground with his finger. When they kept on questioning him, he straightened up and said to them, "Let any one of you who is without sin be the first to throw a stone at her." Again he stooped down and wrote on the ground.
>
> At this, those who heard began to go away one at a time, the older ones first, until only Jesus was left, with the woman still standing there. Jesus straightened up and asked her, "Woman, where are they? Has no one condemned you?"
>
> "No one, sir," she said.
>
> "Then neither do I condemn you," Jesus declared. "Go now and leave your life of sin."
> (John 8:1-11)

4. Why do you suppose the Pharisees wanted to punish this woman?

5. In your own words, what was Jesus' response to their request?

6. Why did the woman's accusers walk away without harming her?

7. Can you draw any parallels to this woman's experience with Jesus and your own? If so, what?

8. Have you ever been on the other side of things—with those who were ready to stone her? If so, what did you learn from that experience?

9. What else from this passage can you apply to your life?

This story is a beautiful picture of God's grace. While this woman, by law, deserved to die, Jesus knew her accusers were guilty of many sins as well. Every person in that crowd deserved punishment.

And that applies to us, too. While our parents might be guilty of sins leading to their divorce, particularly adultery, aren't we all guilty of sin? Have you ever secretly envied your best friend's designer purse? Have you used foul language on the basketball court? These sins might not carry the same consequences as adultery, but they're still sins in God's eyes.

Just as the Pharisees stopped condemning the woman, Jesus wants us to stop condemning our parents for their mistakes. Instead of pointing fingers and wasting your energy on anger and blame, examine your own heart and confess your sins to God.

Take some time now to close in prayer. If adultery was an issue in your parents' marriage, ask God to help you understand how it contributed to their divorce. If you harbor any angry feelings about adultery, confess these to God and ask him to release you from this anger. Write down your prayer.

DAY 2—CRASH AND BURN

Today we'll cover a topic not specifically addressed in the Bible regarding divorce: Abuse. Abuse takes on many forms in a marriage: Physical, verbal, mental, emotional, spiritual, and even stalking. Both men and women are victims of abuse, although women are five to eight times more likely to be abused.[5]

So what exactly is abuse? "*Domestic abuse*, also known as *spousal abuse*, occurs when one person in an intimate relationship or marriage tries to dominate and control the other person" by using intimidation, humiliation, and injury.[6]

Obviously this is not the way God intended for us to treat others, especially our spouses.

If the Bible doesn't specifically address the issue of abuse, then how do we know it's wrong? Because God gave us specific instructions on how we should treat others.

Read Ephesians 5:21-33 and answer the following questions:

"21 Submit to one another out of reverence for Christ.

22 Wives, submit yourselves to your own husbands as you do to the Lord. 23 For the husband is the head of the wife as Christ is the head of the church, his body, of which he is the Savior. 24 Now as the church submits to Christ, so also wives should submit to their husbands in everything.

25 Husbands, love your wives, just as Christ loved the church and gave himself up for her 26 to make her holy, cleansing her by the washing with water through the word, 27 and to present her to himself as a radiant church, without stain or wrinkle or any other blemish, but holy and blameless. 28 In this same way, husbands ought to love their wives as their own bodies. He who loves his wife loves himself. 29 After all, people have never hated their own bodies, but they feed and care for them, just as Christ does the church—30 for we are members of his body. 31 "For this reason a man will leave his father and mother and be united to his wife, and the two will become one flesh." 32 This is a profound mystery—but I am talking about Christ and the church. 33 However, each one of you also must love his wife as he loves himself, and the wife must respect her husband. (Ephesians 5:21-33)

1. How does God want husbands to love and treat their wives? (Ephesians 5:25, 28, 31, 33)

2. How does abuse contradict this type of love?

3. How can a husband demonstrate the Ephesians type of love toward his wife?

4. How does God want a wife to treat her husband according to Ephesians 5:22, 24, 33?

God calls wives to submit to their husbands. The idea of submission is controversial in both Christian and secular circles. Some people believe submission degrades a woman, that it requires her to lose a part of herself. However, that's not the submission God desires. True Christian submission occurs when a wife trusts her husband enough to allow him to spiritually lead the family.

Think about this for a minute: If the husband truly seeks God's will for his family and if he loves his wife with the patience and tenderness in which Christ loved the church, then the wife's responsibility to submit to her husband should be relatively easy.

Now we raise another question: Must the wife submit to her husband if he doesn't love her? Must the husband still love his wife if she refuses to submit? God doesn't play the "what if" game. He only gives us instruction and expects us to follow. We cannot control someone's actions; we can only control our own response to those actions. And our response must always be one of obedience to God. Let's continue to look at how God wants us to treat others.

5. What mutual responsibilities do husbands and wives share according to Ephesians 5:21? Summarize this command in your own words.

Submit to one another out of reverence for Christ. (Ephesians 5:21)

6. How should we treat others, including our spouses? (Ephesians 4:31-32)

Get rid of all bitterness, rage and anger, brawling and slander, along with every form of malice. Be kind and compassionate to one another, forgiving each other, just as in Christ God forgave you. (Ephesians 4:31-32)

7. What does God say about verbal abuse? (Ephesians 4:29)

Do not let any unwholesome talk come out of your mouths, but only what is helpful for building others up according to their needs, that it may benefit those who listen. (Ephesians 4:29)

Abuse is a very personal and painful topic. Sometimes it's easy to recognize. However, the abuse is more difficult to detect when the abuser is manipulative and controlling.

If you've witnessed or sensed abuse in your home, you need to tell someone. This problem is too big for you to handle on your own. Make a list of the reasons why you think abuse has occurred and take it to a trusted teacher, counselor, or church youth worker. God wants you and your family living in a safe, secure environment. Certain people can help you in this situation.

Close in prayer today by asking God to give you a spirit of submission to him. Read Ephesians 4:31-32 again and ask God to help you choose the behaviors that mirror Christ's love. Write down your prayer.

DAY 3—FINAL DEPARTURE

When you hear the word *abandoned*, what picture comes to mind? A creepy, dark warehouse where water trickles down from the barely there ceiling? A mangy, wandering puppy with protruding ribs?

Unfortunately, abandonment is present in many families, and it takes on many forms. Today we'll look at how abandonment contributes to divorce and how you can heal from this painful experience.

Abandonment includes both physical and emotional desertion. Physical abandonment occurs when one person physically leaves another person. This is most common when one spouse moves out of the house.

During my college years, a friend shared with me that her mother arrived home after work one day to a shocking discovery: My friend's father had left her mother and younger sister. Her mother was shocked. His clothes were gone. The TV was missing. The silence and emptiness filled the house. The marriage definitely had problems leading up to the abandonment. But when the father left his home and family, the looming threat of divorce suddenly became official...inevitable...final.

If you can identify with this scenario, then you've probably experienced abandonment. Abandonment occurs when someone leaves with no intention of returning.

The person(s) left behind may be in a weaker, more vulnerable state, but they aren't completely destroyed by the person's absence.[7] After my friend's dad moved out, her mom and sister were more vulnerable because they had to adjust their living standards to accommodate one income. Her sister also lost the sense of safety and security that comes from living with both parents.

Emotional abandonment also occurs in marriage, but it's not as obvious as physical abandonment. It occurs when one person emotionally withdraws, shutting down his or her feelings and stops communicating with the other person.

Physical and emotional abandonment are equally painful and difficult in marriage. Read 1 Corinthians 7:10-16 to gain insight into God's views on abandonment.

10 To the married I give this command (not I, but the Lord): A wife must not separate from her husband. 11 But if she does, she must remain unmarried or else be reconciled to her husband. And a husband must not divorce his wife.

12 To the rest I say this (I, not the Lord): If any brother has a wife who is not a believer and she is willing to live with him, he must not divorce her. 13 And if a woman has a husband who is not a believer and he is willing to live with her, she must not divorce him. 14 For the unbelieving husband has been sanctified through his wife, and the unbelieving wife has been sanctified through her believing husband. Otherwise your children would be unclean, but as it is, they are holy.

15 But if the unbeliever leaves, let it be so. The brother or sister is not bound in such circumstances; God has called us to live in peace. 16 How do you know, wife, whether you

will save your husband? Or, how do you know, husband, whether you will save your wife? (1 Corinthians 7:10-16)

1. Summarize 1 Corinthians 7:10-16 in your own words:

2. Sometimes we raise the issue of believing and non-believing spouses in marriage. According to 1 Corinthians 7:12-13, does God want a believer to divorce a nonbeliever?

_____ Yes   _____ No

Why would God command this? Doesn't he want us married to Christians? Yes. God wants believers to marry other believers so they'll have fruitful, God-honoring marriages. But often after two non-Christians marry, one of the spouses will convert to Christianity—and so what is a new Christian to do if his or her spouse doesn't share the same beliefs? Paul says to stay married—and at least not be the one to call for divorce. Rather the believer's life should be a light and testimony to the non-Christian spouse. In relationships like the one you read about in 1 Corinthians, the believer's positive habits and beliefs can rub off on the unbeliever. Often the unbeliever is drawn to Christ through the believing spouse's witness.

3. What are God's instructions if a nonbeliever abandons a believer? (1 Corinthians 7:15)

When one spouse abandons the other, he violates the marriage covenant he made before God and witnesses. He also misuses the free will God has given him. According to Dr. Jim Denison, pastor of teaching at Park Cities Baptist Church in Dallas, Texas, "The Bible forbids this divorce, but the laws of our land do not. And the Bible clearly teaches that we are not responsible for the sins of others, but only our own."[8]

That's the bottom line. We're responsible for only our own sins.

If we live in God's will and submit to God's authority, we can rest assured God is pleased with us. We cannot control other people's thoughts, actions, or words. We can control only our reactions to them.

When considering the issue of abandonment, don't place the blame on one parent or the other. Instead, focus on your response to the situation. Your attitude should always be one of forgiveness and grace since God forgives us.

If one or both of your parents have abandoned you and the rest of your family, pray that God will help you to forgive them. Remember not to focus on *their actions*, but on *your reactions*. How does God want you to react to this situation? Does he want you to spend time and energy feeling anger, bitterness, resentment, and sadness? Or does he want you to find peace and forgiveness?

I want to stress that you shouldn't stuff or ignore your feelings of anger, bitterness, and the rest. Don't hide your feelings or pretend they don't exist. Rather, take this opportunity to work through your feelings.

Let's close today by confessing to God any feelings of abandonment you might have. If you haven't experienced abandonment, take a moment to pray for those who've suffered through this painful experience. Write down your prayer.

DAY 4—THE NEED FOR SPEED

The tabloids love to splatter pictures of young celebrities partying, drinking, and doing drugs. Given these images, you'd think addiction is a problem reserved for the teenage population. However, "1 in 4 kids under 18 lives in a family where a person abuses alcohol or suffers from alcoholism."[9]

Addiction is a problem that spans all generations.

What Is Addiction?

Addiction is rampant in our society and takes on many forms. So what exactly is addiction? Some people believe it's a physical disease, while others think it's a behavioral problem.

According to About.com—

> "Physically and psychologically, *addiction* has two definitions:
> 1. Having a compulsive physical and psychological need for [something];
> 2. Compulsively engaging in an activity to fill a psychological need that is beyond one's control."[10]

Compulsive is the key word in both of these definitions. Addiction is compulsive, meaning it becomes an obsession. When a person becomes obsessed with something, his overwhelming need for this "something" overtakes his need and desire for the basic necessities of life. People give up their families, friends, and jobs to satisfy their addictions. An addict's sole purpose becomes satisfying his addiction—at any cost.

What Are People Addicted To?

A person may be addicted to a number of things, some seemingly harmless and some more dangerous. People can even develop an addiction to things that seem safe when used in moderation, such as television, video games, shopping, and food. However, these things can overtake one's life and cause just as much destruction and pain as addictions to alcohol, illegal and prescription drugs, tobacco, gambling, and pornography.

How Can I Recognize Addiction?

Read Proverbs 23:29-35 to sneak a peek into the life of an alcoholic.

29 Who has woe? Who has sorrow? Who has strife? Who has complaints? Who has needless bruises? Who has bloodshot eyes?

30 Those who linger over wine, who go to sample bowls of mixed wine.

31 Do not gaze at wine when it is red, when it sparkles in the cup, when it goes down smoothly!

32 In the end it bites like a snake and poisons like a viper.

33 Your eyes will see strange sights and your mind imagine confusing things.

34 You will be like one sleeping on the high seas, lying on top of the rigging.

35 "They hit me," you will say, "but I'm not hurt! They beat me, but I don't feel it! When will I wake up so I can find another drink?" (Proverbs 23:29-35)

1. What words describe the addict's life? (v. 29)

2. What are the damaging effects of alcohol according to verses 32-35?

According to these verses, alcohol affects a person's perception, mind, ability to rest, and ability to feel pain. People escape to alcohol because it numbs their emotions.

3. What's this person's main concern in spite of the downward spiral he experiences? (v. 35)

Can you see how the addiction takes over his life?

How Does Someone Become an Addict?

So how and why does a person become addicted in the first place?[11] The answer is complex and different for each addict. Some people have a genetic predisposition toward addiction. Other people deal with behavioral issues.

People often succumb to addiction while trying to ease their emotional pain. Look at 16-year-old Melissa, for example. Both her sister and her grandfather died in less than a month, her parents fought constantly, and the coach cut her from the high school basketball team.

Melissa felt sad and depressed. No one understood her pain. So she began taking prescription sleeping pills to help her sleep. But Melissa soon realized the emotional pain always returned once she woke up. So she took some antidepressants she found in her parents' medicine cabinet to numb the pain during the day, too. While the drugs allowed her to temporarily avoid her pain, they also prevented her from experiencing the joys in life.

People also become addicts to escape reality. Sometimes life is too painful, too difficult, or too overwhelming for a person to handle. After Joel's parents separated, he moved in with his dad. Then Joel's dad accepted a new job in another state, and he and Joel moved away. Joel missed his mom, his school, and his friends. Adjusting to his new life was so overwhelming that Joel began drinking alcohol when he was alone after school and while his dad was still at work. Drinking allowed Joel to relax and escape the realities of his life.

Finally, people use addiction as a way to control their circumstances. For instance, Kate's mom and dad were both attorneys who worked long hours in large, downtown firms. And they demanded the same dedication and hard work from Kate. So when her GPA fell from a 4.2 to a 4.0, her parents flipped out. When she lost the student council president election, they didn't hide their disappointment. Kate felt like she had no control in her life because her parents called all the shots. The only thing Kate thought she could control was what she ate. She began depriving herself of her favorite foods, and she eventually skipped meals altogether. Her need to please her parents, yet gain independence and control, caused her to develop an eating disorder.

People become addicts for many more reasons, including seeking others' approval, coping with rejection, seeking security and stability, and striving to obtain perfection.

How Does God Want Us to Respond to Addiction?

The Bible doesn't address addiction specifically. However, Christian author Philip Yancey puts addiction in perspective for us:

> *"What the Old Testament calls idolatry, enlightened Westerners call 'addictions.' These, too, are often good things—sex, food, work, chocolate—that outgrow their rightful place and begin to control a person's life."* [12]

God addresses idolatry numerous times in the Bible. Idolatry is the worship of idols. We worship idols in our life anytime someone or something is more important to us than our relationship with Jesus Christ.

If your commitment to watch TV is more important than your commitment to have your daily quiet time, television is your idol. If you skip church and forget to spend time in the Word on Sunday because you're too tired from a Saturday night party, partying is your idol. An idol is anything that takes precedence over your relationship with God.

Let's see what we can learn about addiction from the biblical lessons on idolatry. Colossians 3:5 says, "Put to death, therefore, whatever belongs to your earthly nature: sexual immorality, impurity, lust, evil desires and greed, which is idolatry."

4. In your own words, what does "put to death" mean? How can we put all sin, including addictions, "to death"?

5. The word *lust* is also translated "passion" from the Greek word *pathos*. In this case, "passion" (pathos) means uncontrolled, illegitimate desire.[13] For what things can people have uncontrolled desire?

In Colossians 3:5 the word *greed* comes from the Greek word *pleonexian*, meaning "desire to have more." According to an article written by Dr. Thomas L. Constable, greed is "any materialistic desire including lust that disregards the rights of others. It is 'the arrogant and ruthless assumption that all other persons and things exist for one's own benefit.'"[14] As you can see, greed, which can often lead to addiction, devalues people.

6. What does God say we should do about idolatry and addiction? (1 Corinthians 10:14)

Therefore, my dear friends, flee from idolatry. (1 Corinthians 10:14)

What Should I Do if My Mom or Dad Is an Addict?

After reading the fictitious scenarios above, one or more might seem familiar to you. If you worry that your mom, dad, sibling, or friend has an addiction, write down your concerns. If you're worried about your mom, talk to your dad—and vice versa. If you don't feel comfortable talking to your parents, then talk with a school counselor, teacher, or another trusted adult. Addiction is serious, dangerous, and deadly. You aren't equipped to handle someone's addiction, and it's not your responsibility to do so.

And take a minute to reflect on your own life. Do you feel like addiction might be a problem for you? Do you spend weekend nights drinking? Do you daydream in class, just waiting for the bell to ring so you can leave and smoke a cigarette in the parking lot? If you identify with these examples, you might be struggling with addiction. Please take this seriously and talk to a trusted adult, whether your parents, a counselor, or your youth pastor. They'll provide the resources you need.

Let's spend time in prayer asking God to protect you from addictions. Also, if you think you know someone who is an addict, pray for that person's safety and healing. Write down your prayer.

DAY 5—CAR TROUBLE

You might hear parents say things like, "We just don't have anything in common anymore," "I fell out of love," "I don't know what brought us together in the first place," "We're completely different people," or "We can't agree on anything." Does this sound familiar?

Mrs. Doubtfire, a 1993 film starring Robin Williams and Sally Field, provides a closer look at parents who divorce simply because they no longer get along with each other. During one scene, Miranda (played by Sally Field) explains to her nanny, Mrs. Doubtfire (played by Robin Williams), why she divorced her husband, Daniel (also played by Robin Williams). Miranda explains she fell in love with Daniel because of his humor, spontaneity, and energy; but when the responsibility of kids, careers, and the house piled up, his humor became more of an irritating itch. "I didn't like who I was when I was with him...I would turn into this horrible person...When I'm not with Daniel, I'm better," she said.

As parents change and grow, their needs change and grow as well. If one parent cannot meet the new needs of the other parent, couples will often divorce.

When parents divorce because they've grown apart, there are usually many underlying issues between them. These issues are very complex and differ by marriage. Instead of focusing on the many reasons why your parents couldn't get along, focus on how you can avoid the "we just don't get along anymore" trap in your own relationships.

Love

God wants us to show love to others. By loving others more than ourselves, we can avoid petty arguments. First Corinthians 13:4-7 is read at many weddings, but it applies to *all* relationships. Read this passage and answer the following questions.

Love is patient, love is kind. It does not envy, it does not boast, it is not proud. It does not dishonor others, it is not self-seeking, it is not easily angered, it keeps no record of wrongs.

Love does not delight in evil but rejoices with the truth. It always protects, always trusts, always hopes, always perseveres. (1 Corinthians 13:4-7)

1. According to Paul, what is love?

2. What is love *not*?

3. How has God shown his love to you this past week?

4. How have you shown love to others this week?

5. How have you shown the *opposite* of love to others this past week?

Sympathy and Compassion

6. According to 1 Peter 3:8, how are we to treat others?

Finally, all of you, be like-minded, be sympathetic, love one another, be compassionate and humble. (1 Peter 3:8)

Being sympathetic toward someone doesn't mean you feel sorry for her. It means you cut her some slack; give her the benefit of the doubt; put her feelings and needs before your own. It also implies you help her bear the burden by sharing her feelings.

My husband, Brandon, is a harmonizer. He always gives people the benefit of the doubt. If someone cuts him off on the freeway, he assumes that driver is rushing to the hospital or to another important place. (I assume the driver is paying more attention to his cell phone conversation than his driving.) Brandon always extends sympathy to others, and he often reminds me to show compassion to others as well. His motto is "everyone is having a bad day." This saying reminds me to treat everyone with patience, respect, and compassion.

7. Is there someone in your life who needs sympathy or compassion from you? If so, who is it and how can you minister to that person this week?

Humility

God also wants us to be humble. This requires us to put other people's feelings and needs before our own. God calls us to live in community, but we cannot achieve community if we're always focusing on our own needs first.

We must consider the needs of others as more important than our own.

8. Read Philippians 2:3-4. What are some ways in which you can put someone else's needs, wants, or feelings before your own this week? Will you make the commitment to do this?

Do nothing out of selfish ambition or vain conceit. Rather, in humility value others above yourselves, not looking to your own interests but each of you to the interests of others. (Philippians 2:3-4)

Take some time to think about how your parents treat each other. Do they talk to one another with respect or do they yell at each other and use sarcasm? Are they considerate of each other's time? Do they speak kindly (or at least civilly) about the other parent, or do they go out of their way to complain about their ex-spouse?

9. Make a list of the ways your parents treat each other that bother you.

10. Now make a list of all the ways your parents treat each other that you appreciate and would like to model.

11. Now think about the future for a moment. Someday you might get married. Try to picture what you want your relationship with your spouse to look like. Make a list of things you commit NOT to do in your own marriage.

12. Now make a list of things you promise your future spouse you WILL do in your marriage.

In his book Sacred Marriage, *author Gary Thomas explains his theory on marriage: "What if God designed marriage to make us holy more than to make us happy?"*[15]

This stings many egos because our culture promotes a different philosophy: Just do it. Look out for yourself. Most people spend their lives trying to achieve happiness, not holiness.

Today we talked about love and humility—two vital qualities for making a marriage work. You can prepare yourself for marriage by practicing these virtues with your parents, siblings, and friends.

Take some time today to write a letter to your future spouse. I know marriage seems pretty far in the future, but even today God is preparing your heart for your future mate. Tell that person how you plan to treat him or her in your marriage. Then save this letter for the future. What an amazing gift you'll give to your bride or groom on your wedding day! And your spouse will know that you allowed God to prepare you for marriage since you were a teenager. There is no greater gift you could give someone you love.

GROUP SESSION
WEEK TWO—CRIMES AND MISDEMEANORS
Exploring Reasons for Divorce

GOAL
This week you'll continue the journey by discussing the different reasons why parents divorce and helping students identify why their parents divorced. You'll also take a look at times when God permits divorce.

SUGGESTED ICEBREAKER
You'll need:
• A copy of "Stay Together for the Kids" (*Take Off Your Pants and Jacket*, 2001)
• A CD player"

Let the students listen to "Stay Together for the Kids" by blink-182 (*Take Off Your Pants and Jacket*, 2001). You might want to find the lyrics online and print copies of them so the students can read the words of the song while they listen.

After the song ends, discuss the following questions:

1. What's your reaction to this song?

2. Why do you think the singer's parents divorced?

3. In this situation do you think the singer would have preferred his parents stay together, even though they fought a lot?

4. It's obvious that the singer's parents didn't get along. Besides general disharmony in the marriage, what are some reasons parents divorce?

GROUP DISCUSSION
Ask: When, if at all, does the Bible permit divorce? (*Allow students to offer their ideas.*)

Then continue: Before diving into the current reasons why parents divorce, we must understand how divorce originated. We must also understand God's view of divorce.

Certificate of Divorce

Explain the following ideas to the students:

• God commanded his people to issue a certificate of divorce, but God prefers that no one divorce because it destroys a covenant with God and with another person.

So God created human beings in his own image, in the image of God he created him; male and female he created them. (Genesis 1:27)

For this reason a man will leave his father and mother and be united to his wife, and they will become one flesh. (Genesis 2:24)

"I hate divorce," says the Lord God of Israel, "and I hate it when people clothe themselves with injustice," says the Lord Almighty. So be on your guard, and do not be unfaithful. (Malachi 2:16)

Jesus replied, "Moses permitted you to divorce your wives because your hearts were hard. But it was not this way from the beginning." (Matthew 19:8)

• God knew his people's hearts were hard. God knew they'd divorce anyway.

Some Pharisees came and tested him by asking, "Is it lawful for a man to divorce his wife?"

"What did Moses command you?" he replied.

They said, "Moses permitted a man to write a certificate of divorce and send her away."

"It was because your hearts were hard that Moses wrote you this law," Jesus replied. "But at the beginning of creation God 'made them male and female.' 'For this reason a man will leave his father and mother and be united to his wife, and the two will become one flesh.' So they are no longer two, but one. Therefore what God has joined together, let no one separate." (Mark 10:2-9)

• Therefore, Moses created a certificate of divorce to protect the wife from being accused of adultery, which was punishable by death.[16]

"It has been said, 'Anyone who divorces his wife must give her a certificate of divorce.' " (Matthew 5:31)

WHY DID PEOPLE DIVORCE IN THE OLD TESTAMENT?

There are two schools of thought on this issue:

• Some believe a Jewish man could divorce his wife for any reason, no matter how large or small the issue. These problems included breaking the Jewish laws, as well as things as insignificant as a wife burning her husband's dinner.

"If a man marries a woman who becomes displeasing to him because he finds something indecent about her, and he writes her a certificate of divorce, gives it to her and sends her from his house." (Deuteronomy 24:1)

• Others believe a Jewish man could divorce his wife only if she committed adultery or some other sexual sin.[17]

Jesus replied, "Moses permitted you to divorce your wives because your hearts were hard. But it was not this way from the beginning. I tell you that anyone who divorces his wife, except for sexual immorality, and marries another woman commits adultery." (Matthew 19:8-9)

WHY DO PEOPLE DIVORCE TODAY?

If time permits, ask students to read the following verses aloud and then discuss which reasons contributed to their own parents' divorce. If time doesn't allow for the reading of each Scripture, encourage the students to read these verses during their daily quiet times.

Adultery

"I tell you that anyone who divorces his wife, except for sexual immorality, and marries another woman commits adultery." (Matthew 19:9)

"You shall not commit adultery." (Exodus 20:14, Deuteronomy 5:18)

But a man who commits adultery has no sense; whoever does so destroys himself. (Proverbs 6:32)

Abandonment

But if the unbeliever leaves, let it be so. The brother or sister is not bound in such circumstances; God has called us to live in peace. (1 Corinthians 7:15)

Abuse

Husbands, love your wives, just as Christ loved the church and gave himself up for her. (Ephesians 5:25)

....

If your group meets for 12 weeks, wrap up the session after discussing adultery, abandonment, and abuse and close simply in prayer and be open to any questions from your students. Then pick up the discussion in Week Four by reviewing these reasons.

As an icebreaker for Week Four, ask how they're feeling this week in general. Has anything happened in the past week that has stirred up strong emotions? Use this as a time to allow students to open up, encourage one another, and move to a deeper, more personal level of sharing.

Then begin exploring other reasons why parents divorce. Also discuss some myths of why parents divorce and use the Closing Activity listed here as the Closing Activity for Week Four.

Remind students to read over their Week Three (Chapter Two) homework before you meet again.

....

Ask:

- What are some other reasons why parents divorce?
- What are your thoughts and feelings about why your parents divorced?
- What are some myths about the cause of divorce?

Myth #1—Kids are the cause of divorce. Students need to understand they aren't the cause of their parents' divorce. Sure, kids add stress to any marriage; but the parents are the adults, and they're responsible for their own decisions.

Myth #2—The kids could have done something to prevent the divorce. Many children of divorce believe that if they'd only behaved better, earned better grades, or helped out more around the house, then their parents would not have divorced. Some students also carry the

burden of ignoring issues such as abuse and addiction. These kids need to know that whatever led to their parents' divorce, they aren't responsible for preventing it.

Other myths?

CLOSING ACTIVITY

Play the clip from *Mrs. Doubtfire* in which Miranda (played by Sally Field) explains to Mrs. Doubtfire (played by Robin Williams) why she divorced her husband, Daniel. Then engage the students in a discussion of the questions below:

1. What did Miranda love about Daniel when they first met?

2. What did Miranda dislike about Daniel when they divorced?

3. Why had Miranda's feelings toward Daniel's qualities changed?

4. What's your reaction to her reasons for getting a divorce?

YOU'LL NEED—
• A copy of *Mrs. Doubtfire* (Twentieth Century Fox, 1993), cued to 1:15:20 and end at 1:17:10
• A television or video projection unit
• A DVD player

SWITCHING DRIVERS

Life Changes after Divorce

Divorce brings many life changes for you and your parents. If you like schedules, routine, and order, then these changes might be difficult for you to accept. And if you're a free spirit, then you'll probably have an easier time handling these changes. In either case, we'll spend this week preparing for your new life post-divorce.

DAY 1—THE CLOCK IS TICKING

Whenever I go on a road trip, I find myself constantly looking at the clock. I'm always concerned about the time, schedules, and being punctual. Instead of enjoying the scenery on long drives, I'm usually preoccupied with how fast or slow the time passes. I want to arrive at my destination as quickly as possible. Sometimes the drive drags and 10 minutes seem more like 10 hours. Other times, like when I'm engaged in a great conversation or listening to my favorite music, 10 hours seem like 10 minutes. My attitude greatly influences the time spent in the car.

One of the main changes that occurs as a result of divorce is the amount of time you spend with each parent. Do you bounce between two homes on a weekly basis, giving your parents equal time with you? Or do you spend the majority of your time with one parent? How does your attitude affect the time you spend with your mom and your dad? How can you make the most of your time together?

First of all, consider the time Jesus spent on earth. He lived for 33 years—but his public ministry spanned only the last three years of his life. And look at all he accomplished in that time. Today's average life span in the United States is 77.6 years, so a 33-year-old man is just getting started.[18]

God wants you to make the most of your time on earth, no matter how much or how little time he gives you.

1. If divorce has changed the amount of time you spend with your parents, how do you feel about this? Check all that apply:

❏ Angry	❏ Sad	❏ Happy
❏ Resentful	❏ Indifferent	❏ Relieved
❏ Confused	❏ Bitter	

2. Regarding time, how does Paul instruct us to live according to Ephesians 5:15-16?

Be very careful, then, how you live—not as unwise but as wise, making the most of every opportunity, because the days are evil. (Ephesians 5:15-16)

3. What does Paul teach in Galatians 6:10?

Therefore, as we have opportunity, let us do good to all people, especially to those who belong to the family of believers. (Galatians 6:10)

4. How can you apply these verses to spending time with your parents?

Do you feel like your parents give you enough of their time and attention? If not, then you might be tempted to rebel against them. But God doesn't want you do that—God wants you (and all of us) to behave with love.

But God doesn't want you to lose your temper. God wants you to respond in love and maturity. Unfortunately, your parents might not realize there's been a drastic shift in the amount of time they spend with you. It's not because they don't love you, because they do. They're simply adjusting to new schedules, new jobs, new routines, and new relationships, just like you are.

So how should you handle this? If you have concerns, share them with your parents. Here are some suggestions you can make that might help you spend more time together:

• Everyone needs to eat, right? Determine a reasonable number of nights to eat dinner to-gether. If school activities or your parent's job prevent this, then try eating breakfast together. What about indulging in a dessert or coffee at your favorite café a couple nights a week?

• What hobbies do you share? Schedule time to do these things together. Are you both runners? Wake up early two to three mornings each week and run together. Do you have a pet? Take your dog to a weekly pet obedience class. This benefits everyone in the family, even Fido.
• Is there nothing good to watch on TV? Turn it off. Yes, this is a radical idea, but it works. And while you're at it, turn off the computer, mp3 player, stereo, and cell phone, too. Take just 30 minutes to catch up on what's going on in each other's lives.

Sometimes our problem isn't a lack of time, but how we choose to spend it.

Take a few minutes to brainstorm some more ideas for ways you and your parents can spend more one-on-one time together.

1.

2.

3.

4.

5.

Make a commitment to do one of these things with your parents this week. You won't regret the time you spend together.
Let's take a moment to close in prayer.

Dear God,

Thank you for the gift of time. I pray you'll help me to use my time wisely. Help me not to waste it, but take advantage of it by investing in the people around me. I pray you'll give my parents and me more time to spend together. Help us to know how to use this time to grow closer to each other and to you. Amen.

DAY 2—MONEY, MONEY, MONEY

One of the most visible changes that occurs in a divorce is finances. Stay-at-home moms must suddenly become career women. Two-income families divide into two single-income families. Parents pay lawyers' fees, court costs, moving costs, and so on. These expenses add up, and the family's budget tightens. Everyone, including the kids, feels the changes in income.

When my mom divorced her second husband, our financial situation changed dramatically. We moved out of a plush 4,000 square foot home (complete with four bedrooms, three and a half bathrooms, two living rooms, two dens, and a maid's quarters) into a small, two-bedroom, one-bath house in serious need of repairs. My mom, who'd always worked before remarrying, had taken on the role of stay-at-home mom during her second marriage. So when she divorced, she had to rejoin the workforce.

During and after this divorce, I worried about many things, including money. How would we pay our rent? How would my mom pay for my school activities? Would I get a car when I turned 16? I hadn't even thought about the bigger question—How would I pay for college? We were focused on day-to-day survival, and the financial strain caused a great deal of stress for my mom and I. Yet, like many single mothers, she sacrificed many things and worked hard so she could pay for my cheerleading uniforms, camp, and school clothes.

1. Have you noticed a drastic shift in your family's finances since the divorce? If so, list some ways in which financial change has affected your life.

2. Now take the time to write down a few things that worry you regarding finances. Are you worried your parents won't be able to send you to summer camp? Are you worried about paying for college? List anything that's weighing on your heart.

If you think back to Week One, you might remember reading Matthew 6:25-34. This passage talks about finances and what God desires regarding our attitudes toward money. Take a minute to re-read this passage and then answer the following questions.

25 "Therefore I tell you, do not worry about your life, what you will eat or drink; or about your body, what you will wear. Is not life more important than food, and the body more important than clothes? 26 Look at the birds of the air; they do not sow or reap or store away in barns, and yet your heavenly Father feeds them. Are you not much more valuable than they? 27 Who of you by worrying can add a single hour to his life?

28 And why do you worry about clothes? See how the flowers of the field grow. They do not labor or spin. 29 Yet I tell you that not even Solomon in all his splendor was dressed like one of these. 30 If that is how God clothes the grass of the field, which is here today and tomorrow is thrown into the fire, will he not much more clothe you—you of little faith? 31 So do not worry, saying, 'What shall we eat?' or 'What shall we drink?' or 'What shall we wear?' 32 For the pagans run after all these things, and your heavenly Father knows that you need them. 33 But seek first his kingdom and his righteousness, and all these things will be given to you as well. 34 Therefore do not worry about tomorrow, for tomorrow will worry about itself. Each day has enough trouble of its own." (Matthew 6:25-34)

3. What does Jesus command his disciples to do (or not to do) in verse 25?

4. Verse 25 tells us *what* we should do, but verses 26-27 tell us why we should do it. Explain the *why* of Jesus' command.

First, Jesus tells his disciples they shouldn't worry about material things. Then he tells them why: Because material things are such a small, insignificant part of life. Our relationships with Jesus and with people are more valuable than material things.

This is a tough concept to grasp in our Western culture. Here in the United States, people worship celebrities, clothes, and cars.

We buy houses we cannot afford and rack up credit-card debt to pay for vacations and jewelry. Have you noticed any of these behaviors and choices made in your own family or in your friends' families? People who behave in such ways are putting more confidence in their possessions than in Jesus. They put more trust in material things than in their salvation.

Second, Jesus reassured the disciples he'll provide for their needs by comparing them to birds. Why? Because baby birds are dependent on their parents for food. If the mother or father bird doesn't provide food, then the baby bird will die in the nest.

This message is significant for children of divorce because sometimes after a divorce, parents are unable or unwilling to provide the material things their kids want or need. Yet we should remember Jesus' promise—God will provide for our needs.

Now ask yourself this: Are the things you worry about wants (e.g., the latest Prada handbag, a new baseball glove, or a senior trip to New York City), or are they needs (food, clothing, a place to live, and love)? God doesn't promise to provide everything we *want*; rather, God will give us everything we *need*.

Just in case you still don't believe him, Jesus makes the argument that if God takes care of little birds, God will certainly take care of the humans for which he sent his Son to die.

Check out Luke 12:22-34:

22 Then Jesus said to his disciples: "Therefore I tell you, do not worry about your life, what you will eat; or about your body, what you will wear. 23 Life is more than food, and the body more than clothes. 24 Consider the ravens: They do not sow or reap, they have no storeroom or barn; yet God feeds them. And how much more valuable you are than birds! 25 Who of you by worrying can add a single hour to your life? 26 Since you cannot do this very little thing, why do you worry about the rest?

27 Consider how the wild flowers grow. They do not labor or spin. Yet I tell you, not even Solomon in all his splendor was dressed like one of these. 28 If that is how God clothes the grass of the field, which is here today, and tomorrow is thrown into the fire, how much more will he clothe you—you of little faith! 29 And do not set your heart on what you will eat or drink; do not worry about it. 30 For the pagan world runs after all such things, and your Father knows that you need them. 31 But seek his kingdom, and these things will be given to you as well.

32 Do not be afraid, little flock, for your Father has been pleased to give you the kingdom. 33 Sell your possessions and give to the poor. Provide purses for yourselves that will not wear out, a treasure in heaven that will never fail, where no thief comes near and no moth destroys. 34 For where your treasure is, there your heart will be also." (Luke 12:22-34)

Why does Jesus mention ravens instead of robins or bluebirds? Because ravens are notorious for not providing food for their offspring. Yet Jesus tells us even the ravens aren't doomed to die of starvation because God takes care of them when they're too young and weak to provide for themselves.[19] Therefore, if God takes care of the raven, then he'll take care of our needs as well.

5. In verse 30, Jesus gives us another reason why it's wrong to worry about material things. What does he say?

Jesus tells his disciples that worry is a pagan pastime. (Pagans were people who worshiped false gods and practiced sorcery and other evil customs). As Christians, we're to set ourselves apart from pagans. Pagans worry, yet we're called to trust in God to provide for our needs. When we truly believe God gives us all we need, there is no need to worry.

6. What should you do when you catch yourself worrying about money? (v. 31)

What does it mean to seek his kingdom? Jesus means we should think about eternal things and consider how we can invest in God's kingdom.

> Finally, brothers and sisters, whatever is true, whatever is noble, whatever is right, whatever is pure, whatever is lovely, whatever is admirable—if anything is excellent or praiseworthy—think about such things. Whatever you have learned or received or heard from me, or seen in me—put it into practice. And the God of peace will be with you. (Philippians 4:8-9)

If we think about eternal things, we'll strive toward eternal things.

If we think about temporary, material things, we'll strive to obtain material things. God wants us to use our time and energy on things that will last.

Yes, your family's financial situation will probably change when your parents divorce. Yet God still wants you to trust him. God knows the desires of your heart and will provide them for you.

So how can you adapt to these changes in your family's finances? First, think about how you can help out at home. If your family is used to hiring someone to clean your house, try doing more chores so your family can save on this expense. If you usually buy your lunch at school, pack a lunch instead. You'll not only save money, but you'll probably eat healthier, too.

Second, consider taking on a part-time job or babysitting on the weekends. These are just small ways that you can chip in and help your family adjust to the financial changes.

Finally, lower your expectations. Maybe you received 20 CDs last Christmas. This year, ask your mom for only five. Consider the financial strain and try to make wise decisions that will help your family.

Now take the time to pray and let God know about your worries regarding money and your family's finances. Then pray for the strength and faith to trust God to care and provide for all of your *needs*. Write down this prayer.

DAY 3—MOVING DAY

Zach watched the moving van pull out of the driveway as he and his mom followed behind in their SUV. The weather fit Zach's mood perfectly—gloomy, dreary, and cool. He sat in the backseat with his headphones on, thinking about all the things he was leaving behind: His spot on the varsity soccer team, his role as class vice president, and the group of friends he'd known since kindergarten. This could possibly be the worst day of his life—even worse than the day he found out about his parents' divorce.

Does this story hit too close to home? Divorce brings about many changes, often including a move to a new house, a new school, and sometimes even a new city or state. So how can we deal with these changes that seem so difficult and unfair?

Before we examine our own actions, let's look into the book of Ruth for guidance. Most of our time today will be spent reading this book, so take the time to read it in its entirety. It's only four chapters long, so don't feel overwhelmed. It's worth the read! After reading Ruth, answer the questions below.

1. Why did Ruth move from Moab to Judah? (Ruth 1:3-7)

Now Elimelek, Naomi's husband, died, and she was left with her two sons. They married Moabite women, one named Orpah and the other Ruth. After they had lived there about ten years, both Mahlon and Kilion also died, and Naomi was left without her two sons and her husband.

> When Naomi heard in Moab that the Lord had come to the aid of his people by providing food for them, she and her daughters-in-law prepared to return home from there. With her two daughters-in-law she left the place where she had been living and set out on the road that would take them back to the land of Judah. (Ruth 1:3-7)

It's important to know the cultural background of this story. In Ruth's day when a husband died, the son was in charge of caring for his widowed mother. So when Naomi's husband died, she thankfully had two sons to care for her. However, when both of her sons died, Naomi was left destitute. Women who didn't have a man to care for them were considered the lowest beings in their culture. They often became beggars or prostitutes just to earn enough money to eat.

Ruth and her sister-in-law, Orpah, were in a difficult position as well. When a young woman's husband died, it was customary for her to marry her husband's brother. Then they would have children together, and their firstborn would be considered her first husband's child and earn his inheritance. In this case, however, both brothers died, leaving Ruth and Orpah without a backup plan.

2. Why was it so courageous for Ruth to go with Naomi to Judah?

3. What do you think Ruth was thinking and feeling on her moving day?

If you've ever moved to a new town, then you can identify with what Ruth must have been thinking and feeling. She was probably nervous and scared because she was traveling to an unfamiliar place—a place where she had no friends or family. She didn't know how she'd work, what she'd eat, or where she'd live. But she had faith that God would provide for her needs. And she felt a duty to stay with Naomi and look after her.

4. If you're facing a move, or if your family has recently moved, write down your feelings about this change.

Tomorrow we'll finish our study on Ruth and discover how God continued to bless her faith and obedience. For now, pray that God will help you adjust to your new move. Pray that God would surround you with godly friends in this new place. Write down your prayer.

DAY 4—MOVING DAY (CONTINUED)

Yesterday we began studying the book of Ruth. We looked at how Ruth's upheaval in moving from the land of Moab to Judah parallels our own experiences of moving to a new town. Today we'll continue to look at how God blessed Ruth and how God can bless us in a new place.

Did you notice Ruth's attitude throughout her transition? From the moment Ruth agreed to move to Judah with Naomi, she possessed a positive, supportive attitude. She never complained, whined, or felt sorry for herself.

But her situation is different from mine, you might think. *Ruth had a choice. I don't. It's so unfair!*

Think about Ruth's situation for a moment. The circumstances that led her to move to Judah were also unfair. Her husband's death was unfair. Her culture denying her an adequate job was unfair. Leaving her friends and life behind was unfair.

1. Instead of dwelling on what was unfair in her life, how did Ruth respond to her situation?

2. Think about your own situation. Have you had a "poor me" attitude? Have you been treating your parents disrespectfully because you're angry about the move? Have you given them the silent treatment? Have you already started isolating yourself from your friends? Be honest with yourself and write about your attitude and actions regarding the changes taking place in your life.

3. Are you honoring God with your attitude? How so?

4. If not, what can you do to change your attitude and actions to reflect your faith and trust in God?

When I was a junior in high school, my family moved from a small town to a large city. Six months later we moved to another large city. Two new cities and three high schools in one year was a difficult adjustment. And I admit I didn't always have a positive attitude during that time. I was sad, scared, and angry.

Yet looking at my situation now, I can see how God protected me and provided for me in several ways.

First, God always surrounded me with Christian friends. As the new kid in town, the temptation to fall in with the "wrong crowd" is easy. Everyone wants to belong to a group, even if that group isn't a positive influence. And, unfortunately, sometimes non-Christians are more accepting than Christians. However, in my experience God brought faithful, godly friends into my life in every place I lived.

Second, God provided me with positive activities and interests. I played tennis and was a cheerleader, so this gave me an instant group of friends. It also gave me weekly activities to attend and goals to reach.

Finally, each high school I attended offered Christian fellowship. Young Life, Fellowship of Christian Athletes, Campus Life, and on-campus Bible studies provided me with sound biblical teaching and new friendships. Does your school offer these things? If not, consider starting a Bible study or prayer group. You'll be surprised to discover how many people are also looking for Christian fellowship. (And of course, getting involved in your church youth group can't hurt, either!)

Yesterday we discussed the difficulty a single woman in Ruth's day experienced. However, in today's reading we'll see how God clearly provided a safe, honorable job for Ruth that provided enough food for both her and her mother-in-law.

5. In Ruth 2:1-3, Ruth discovers a way in which she can provide for herself and Naomi. What does she do?

Now Naomi had a relative on her husband's side, a man of standing from the clan of Elimelek, whose name was Boaz.

And Ruth the Moabite said to Naomi, "Let me go to the fields and pick up the leftover grain behind anyone in whose eyes I find favor."

Naomi said to her, "Go ahead, my daughter."

So she went out, entered a field and began to glean behind the harvesters. As it turned out, she found herself working in a field belonging to Boaz, who was from the clan of Elimelek. (Ruth 2:1-3)

6. God not only provided a job for Ruth, but he also blessed her faith and hard work. How does God bless her (Ruth 2:8-18)?

So Boaz said to Ruth, "My daughter, listen to me. Don't go and glean in another field and don't go away from here. Stay here with the women who work for me. Watch the field where the harvesters are working, and follow along after the women. I have told the men not to lay a hand on you. And whenever you are thirsty, go and get a drink from the water jars the men have filled."

At this, she bowed down with her face to the ground. She asked him, "Why have I found such favor in your eyes that you notice me—a foreigner?"

Boaz replied, "I've been told all about what you have done for your mother-in-law since the death of your husband—how you left your father and mother and your homeland and came to live with a people you did not know before. May the Lord repay you for what you have done. May you be richly rewarded by the Lord, the God of Israel, under whose wings you have come to take refuge."

"May I continue to find favor in your eyes, my lord," she said. "You have reassured me and have spoken kindly to your servant—though I do not have the standing of one of your servants."

At mealtime Boaz said to her, "Come over here. Have some bread and dip it in the wine vinegar."

When she sat down with the harvesters, he offered her some roasted grain. She ate all she wanted and had some left over. As she got up to glean, Boaz gave orders to his men, "Let her gather among the sheaves and don't reprimand her. Even pull out some stalks for her from the bundles and leave them for her to pick up, and don't rebuke her."

So Ruth gleaned in the field until evening. Then she threshed the barley she had gathered, and it amounted to about an ephah. She carried it back to town, and her mother-in-law saw how much she had gathered. Ruth also brought out and gave her what she had left over after she had eaten enough. (Ruth 2:8-18)

God blessed Ruth beyond her expectations. Do you think Ruth expected to find such a profitable job when she left Moab? Do you think she anticipated a man like Boaz would treat her with such kindness? Do you think she ever dreamed of remarrying? Probably not.

That's exactly why God's blessings are so amazing—because they are completely unexpected! Ruth responded to her difficult situation with faith and love. God responded to Ruth by protecting, caring for, and providing for her.

Consider these ways in which you can respond to your situation with as much grace as Ruth did:

Introduce yourself to people. Starring as the new kid is intimidating even for the most outgoing personality. Take opportunities at lunch, in the library, or in class to introduce yourself to the people around you. You never know; they might be just as shy as you are.

Jump into your old activities. If you played on the basketball team at your old school, try out for the team at your new school. If you don't make the team or it's not basketball season, then join a community league.

Explore new activities. Maybe you always wanted to write for the school newspaper, but your old school didn't have one. Take the opportunity to join the newspaper staff at your new school.

Meet your neighbors. You just might find a new friend down the street.

God wants you to succeed wherever you live.

Take the time to pray about specific concerns you have regarding moving. Then ask God to provide for each of these concerns. Remember, God provided for Ruth when she moved to Judah. God provided for me in each new city I moved to. God will provide for you, too. Write down your prayer.

DAY 5—FAMILY TIES

We spent this week discussing ways in which our lives change when our parents divorce. While there are many changes that are out of our control—finances, moving, changing schools—there are many changes that are within our control, including our attitudes and actions.

1. When parents split up, the family dynamics shift. People assume different roles than the ones they played before the divorce. Take a moment to think about your life before the divorce. What was your daily routine?

2. Since your parents' divorce, how has that routine changed?

After divorce, everyone in the family adjusts to changes. Let's consider some healthy and unhealthy ways in which our roles change.

Caretaker

Rachel wakes up daily at 5:45 a.m. She folds a load of laundry, packs everyone's lunches, and then wakes her younger brother and sister. As they get ready for school, she hurriedly cooks breakfast and takes a quick shower. She drives to school, too exhausted to concentrate on the day ahead. After school she works a couple of hours at her local dry cleaners. Her dad usually arrives home from work around 6:30 p.m. He suffers from depression and spends the rest of the evening in his room watching TV until he drifts off to sleep. Rachel begins cooking dinner for her family the minute she arrives home. After dinner, she helps her siblings with their homework and then gets them ready for bed. She tackles her own homework and then finally drifts to sleep around midnight.

Rachel's schedule is draining. She carries the bulk of responsibility around the house because her dad is incapable of dealing with reality. She feels responsible for everyone's well being. If they feel sick, she takes care of them. If they feel sad, she comforts them. Rachel feels much older than her real age. She rarely has time to hang out with her friends, and she doesn't participate in any activities outside of school and work.

Does this scenario sound familiar to you? If you can relate to Rachel's day, then you've assumed the role of the caretaker in your family. While I applaud your selfless nature and efforts to help out at home, I want you to take a look at your life. You're currently living the life of an adult, yet you're only a teenager.

A fine line exists between helping your parents around the house and becoming the parent of the house.

As the child, resist the temptation to carry the emotional burdens in the family. Also, try not to worry about the financial changes. Getting a part-time job so you can pay for your own car insurance is a great idea, but worrying about money to the point where you drop all extracurricular activities is not a good idea.

If you feel overwhelmed by your responsibilities, make a list of all your duties. Then take this list to your parents. Let them know you'd like to lighten your load. Review the list with them to determine if there are responsibilities they or another family member can assume instead. You're only one person; so don't feel like you need to do the work of four people.

Best Friends

Jessica's mom, Ms. Wilder, recently began borrowing clothes from Jessica's closet. She also hangs out in Jessica's room whenever Jessica has friends over, and she constantly asks Jessica for the latest gossip. Ms. Wilder allows Jessica to go to rowdy high school parties and has even offered to buy alcohol for Jessica and her friends. Ms. Wilder is clearly more interested in being Jessica's best friend than her mom.

When you first read this story, you might think, *How cool! I wish my mom was like that!* But truthfully, you have hundreds—maybe even thousands—of people at your school who can be your best friend. But only one person can be your mom, and only one can be your dad.

If you recognize any of these behaviors in your parents, have a talk with them. Let them know your concerns. Encourage them to join a book club, Bible study, or another group with people their own age. Chances are they just might be lonely as they adjust to the single life.

Independent

Alex lives with his mom, a commercial real estate developer who travels 75 percent of the time. When she's in town, she devotes most of her time to networking at various community social events. Alex juggles schoolwork, the varsity track team, and a part-time job with no direction from his mom. He feels pressured to succeed, but he doesn't feel like he can go to his mom for advice because she's so busy with her own life. Alex and his mom are too busy for family dinners, and she rarely attends his track meets. He knows her life is hectic and she has enough on her mind without worrying about him. Most of the time he feels lonely, but he could never tell his mom.

If Alex's story mirrors your own, you probably feel very independent, which can be a good thing. However, the downside to being too independent too soon is you also feel very lonely. Can you identify with any of the following?

- There is no one around to take care of me, so I need to take care of myself.
- I rarely see my mom and dad. And when we do spend time together, they feel distant. They have no idea what's going on in my life, but they don't even realize it.
- I have to succeed: If I fail, no one will rescue me.
- I can't wait to be an adult so I can take care of myself and be completely independent.
- I make major decisions, such as which college to attend, without my parents' input.
- My mom and dad are too busy, too stressed, too tired, or too overwhelmed to care about my day-to-day life.

If you can relate to any of those thoughts, consider talking to your parents about how you feel. Let them know how they could be more involved in your life. Also let them know ways in which they can help you. Many parents recognize an independent child and want to give him or her room to grow. However, sometimes parents back off too much. Let your mom and dad know you need them to guide you through these years.

Many parents find that rebuilding their lives post-divorce is more difficult than they anticipated. They need to create new routines and new traditions, adjust to new jobs and new living situations, and even begin dating again. These new experiences can be overwhelming. But that doesn't mean you should carry your parents' responsibilities.

God draws a clear picture of what our roles as parents and children should look like. Let's take a look.

3. According to the following verses, how are children supposed to react to their parents?

- Proverbs 3:1

My son, do not forget my teaching, but keep my commands in your heart. (Proverbs 3:1)

- Proverbs 4:1

Listen, my sons, to a father's instruction; pay attention and gain understanding. (Proverbs 4:1)

• Deuteronomy 5:16

Honor your father and your mother, as the Lord your God has commanded you, so that you may live long and that it may go well with you in the land the Lord your God is giving you. (Deuteronomy 5:16)

4. How does God want parents to treat their children according to the following verses?

• Proverbs 19:18

Discipline your children, for in that there is hope; do not be a willing party to their death. (Proverbs 19:18)

• Deuteronomy 11:18-21

Fix these words of mine in your hearts and minds; tie them as symbols on your hands and bind them on your foreheads. Teach them to your children, talking about them when you sit at home and when you walk along the road, when you lie down and when you get up. Write them on the doorframes of your houses and on your gates, so that your days and the days of your children may be many in the land that the Lord swore to give your ancestors, as many as the days that the heavens are above the earth. (Deuteronomy 11:18-21)

• Ephesians 6:4

Fathers, do not exasperate your children; instead, bring them up in the training and instruction of the Lord. (Ephesians 6:4)

God makes clear his plan for you and your parents. God wants your parents to discipline you because they love you. God wants them to find true joy in raising you. God also wants them to serve as godly examples for you. Finally, God wants your parents to encourage you, not to frustrate you or make you angry. Obviously, God has placed parents in the leadership role.

You have an entirely different role to play. God commands you to listen to your parents. Not only must you listen to their instruction, but you must also apply it to your lives (assuming their advice doesn't defy God's Word). Finally, you must honor and respect your parents.

If you have concerns about your role in the new family dynamics, talk to your parents about it. Let them know what makes you uncomfortable and discuss ways you can change things so you're free to be a kid and let them handle the adult responsibilities.

GROUP SESSION
WEEK THREE—SWITCHING DRIVERS
Life Changes after Divorce

GOAL
This week you'll discuss life changes the students might experience after their parents divorce.

SUGGESTED ICEBREAKER
You'll need:
- A copy of "Wonderful" (*Songs from an American Movie, Vol. 1: Learning How to Smile*, 2000)
- A CD player"

Let the students listen to "Wonderful" by Everclear (*Songs from an American Movie, Vol. 1: Learning How to Smile*, 2000). You might want to find the lyrics online and print copies of them so the students can read the words of the song while they listen.

After the song ends, discuss the following questions:

1. What changes have occurred in the singer's life since his parents divorced?

2. How does he feel about these changes?

GROUP DISCUSSION
The students' homework for Week Three focuses on changes they might experience after their parents' divorce. During the Group Session this week, we want to accomplish the following:

- Discuss the life changes students experience
- Discuss the students' reactions to these changes
- Explore the healthy and unhealthy behaviors that can occur in response to these life changes
- Encourage students to choose positive responses to these life changes

These students are standing at a crossroads. The decisions they make today regarding their behaviors, attitudes, and reactions will affect their lives not only today, but also in the years ahead.

Discuss the following questions:

1. What life changes are out of your control?
• Moving to a different house, city, state

  -If your family has moved, how do you feel about this?
  -What do you miss about your old life?
  -What do you like about your new life?

• Changing schools

  -What's been the most challenging aspect of attending a new school?
  -What do you like most about your new school?
  -How has God taken care of you at your new school?

• Spending equal amounts of time with each parent

  -Do you get frustrated with the amount of time you spend with each of your parents, or do you think the arrangement is fair? Why or why not?

• Financial changes

  -How have you had to adjust to financial changes in your family?
  -What can you do to alleviate the stress on your parents in this area?

• A stay-at-home parent getting a job outside the home

  -Was your mom or dad a stay-at-home parent and is now working outside the home?
  -How has this affected your family?
  -How can you help your family adjust to this change?

• Parents remarrying

  -Have your mom or dad started dating or have they remarried?
  -Whether yes or no, how do you feel about this?

• Bringing new stepsiblings into the family

-If you have stepsiblings, describe the challenges you've faced in dealing with them.
-Describe the blessings of having new brothers and sisters in your family.

• What are some other life changes you've experienced?

2. What life changes are (somewhat) within your control?

• Choosing how you spend time with your parents

-How can you make the most of the time you spend with each parent?

• Calling your parents to keep them updated on your schoolwork, activities, and so on

• Sharing your thoughts and feelings with your parents

-What are some things you want to talk to your parents about regarding the divorce?
-Why haven't you brought this up with your parents?
-What can you do to overcome this hurdle?

....

If your group meets for 12 weeks, wrap up the session after discussing the latter life changes and close simply in prayer and be open to any questions from your students. When you meet again in Week Six, review the life changes they might experience, then tackle the rest of the questions slated for this session.

As an icebreaker for Week Six, ask how they're feeling this week in general. Has anything happened in the past week that has stirred up strong emotions? Use this as a time to allow students to open up, encourage one another, and move to a deeper, more personal level of sharing.

Use the Closing Activity listed here as the Closing Activity for Week Six.

Remind your students to read over their Week Five (Chapter Three) homework before you meet again.

....

In the students' Week Three Bible study, they looked at ways in which they could control their attitudes and reactions to their parents' divorce. Thinking back to that portion of the study, engage the students in the following questions.

Briefly explain each behavior listed below and then ask the questions that follow. The students already explored these unhealthy ways of dealing with life changes during their independent Bible study, so they should be able to engage in the discussion questions. You might want to read aloud one or all of the hypothetical stories from Day Five.

Unhealthy Reactions to Divorce and Life Changes

- Becoming the caretaker
- Becoming best friends with mom or dad
- Becoming too independent

1. Have you adopted any of these behaviors? If so, why?

2. How has this behavior added stress to your life?

3. What do you wish you could change about your current way of dealing with your parents' divorce?

Some other unhealthy ways teenagers may react to their parents' divorce include retreating, rebelling, and taking sides. These behaviors weren't discussed in the Student Guide, so you'll need to briefly describe each behavior, including the dangers that are associated with it and the healthy alternative ways of living. Then ask the students to answer the questions that follow each behavior.

Retreating

- Characteristics

    -Students revert to late elementary school or middle school in terms of their dress, hobbies, interests, and so on.
    -Students isolate themselves from friends and family, often spending the majority of their time alone in their rooms.
    -Students might become more emotionally dependent on family, almost clingy.

- Dangers

    -This type of behavior prevents students from engaging in age-appropriate life experiences and activities.

-Parents resist giving their children new freedoms and responsibilities when they witness this type of behavior. Age-appropriate responsibilities are necessary for proper maturity and development.

• Alternatives

-Teenagers shouldn't build up emotional walls to keep others out. Suggest they find someone with whom they can talk about their feelings.
-Encourage students to keep a journal of their feelings and thoughts.
-Encourage students to embrace their future and the exciting challenges and responsibilities ahead.

Ask:

1. Have you retreated in order to avoid dealing with your emotions about your parents' divorce?

2. How can you begin to open up to others about what you're feeling?

Encourage students to commit to one of the alternative behaviors. They don't need to tell the group which one, they need to make this commitment only to themselves.

Rebelling

• Characteristics

-This behavior is usually the most easily recognized and quickly addressed by parents, which is why students resort to it—it brings them the attention they desire.
-Rebellious students disobey and manipulate their parents, teachers, or even the law.
-Students conflict with their parents in order to separate from them.
-Students take advantage of their newfound freedom. Children raised in single-parent homes generally have more independence and less supervision because their parents work.
-Students can either choose to use this freedom for good (by using their free time wisely in school, work, and activities) or for evil (by killing time after school with drugs and alcohol).

• Dangers

-Students find themselves in dangerous situations dealing with alcohol, drugs, sex, shoplifting, and so on.

-They lose privileges and their parents' respect.

• Alternatives

-Choose positive activities (volunteering, working a part-time job, joining a school organization or sport) instead of negative ones (drinking, smoking, cutting class).
-Accept the fact that rebellious behavior won't reunite your parents.

1. Are you tempted to rebel or have you already started rebelling? If so, why?

2. What can you do to avoid temptation?

Taking Sides

• Characteristics

-Students often leverage one parent in order to get something from the other parent. (For example, "Dad bought me a new Xbox game. Can't I have an Xbox at your house, too?")
-They give one parent the cold shoulder when they don't get what they want.
-Students often give more love, respect, or attention to one parent instead of the other.

• Dangers

-This behavior is hurtful to parents.
-Parents often recognize manipulation and most likely won't give in.
-This behavior continues into adulthood, and students will rely on such tactics to succeed in college, careers, and relationships.

• Alternatives

-Don't choose a "favorite" parent.
-Don't manipulate your parents in order to get things you want (new clothes, a later curfew, a new car, and so on).

1. Do you show favoritism between your parents? If so, how?

2. What can you do to treat them equally?

CLOSING ACTIVITY

Play a clip from *A Walk to Remember* starring Shane West and Mandy Moore. It begins with Jamie (Moore) telling Landon (West) that she has cancer and she's dying. Continue playing the movie through the scene in which Landon asks his dad (a doctor who's divorced from Landon's mom) to help her. End the clip after Landon drives all night and arrives at his home in the morning. Engage students in a discussion using the following questions:

> **YOU'LL NEED—**
> • A copy of *A Walk to Remember* (Warner Bros., 2002), cued to 1:09:13 and end at 1:13:10
> • A television or video projection unit
> • A DVD player

1. How does Landon's life seem to have changed since his parents divorced?
   a. His dad is probably remarried or has a girlfriend, as you see her step out onto the front porch in her bathrobe. Landon's mom, meanwhile, is still single.
   b. His dad lives in a larger, nicer home than where Landon and his mom live.
   c. Judging by the distance Landon drove, his dad seems to live in another city or community.
   d. Landon doesn't seem to have a close relationship with his dad.
   e. Landon doesn't have regular visitation with his dad.

2. What are Landon's feelings toward his dad?
   a. He's angry with his dad.
   b. He assumes he can't count on his dad for support.
   c. He wants to believe his dad will come through for him, yet he seems to have already given up on his dad.

DRIVER'S EDUCATION

How to Effectively Communicate with Your Parents

Communication is difficult for many people, including your parents. Just because they're adults doesn't mean they have this communication thing figured out. This week we'll look at ways you can improve communication with your parents. You'll not only feel better, but chances are you'll both get what you want in the end.

DAY 1—AVOIDING CONFUSION BEHIND THE WHEEL

If you have your driver's license or are learning to drive, you understand the value of communication. Lights, signs, and markers all communicate different things to us on the road. Red means stop, yellow means yield, and green means go. The flashing light in a school zone means we need to drive 20 miles per hour. An ambulance whizzing past with its lights flashing demands we pull over to the shoulder. We know these things because we studied the rules and procedures in driver's ed.

But what if there was no standard for communicating on the road? What if signs and lights didn't exist on the streets? We'd experience more fatalities, wrecks, and chaos, not to mention the fact that we'd probably never get to where we needed to go.

God wants us to clearly communicate with one another so we can carry out his purpose for our lives.

Communication also protects us from danger. In Genesis 11, we'll read a story about a group of people who clearly defied God, so God chose to punish them by taking away their means of communication.

Take a few minutes to read the story of the tower of Babel in Genesis 11:1-9.

> 1 Now the whole world had one language and a common speech. 2 As people moved eastward, they found a plain in Shinar and settled there. 3 They said to each other, "Come, let's make bricks and bake them thoroughly."
>
> They used brick instead of stone, and tar for mortar. 4 Then they said, "Come, let us build

ourselves a city, with a tower that reaches to the heavens, so that we may make a name for ourselves and not be scattered over the face of the whole earth."

5 But the Lord came down to see the city and the tower that they were building. 6 The Lord said, "If as one people speaking the same language they have begun to do this, then nothing they plan to do will be impossible for them. 7 Come, let us go down and confuse their language so they will not understand each other."

8 So the Lord scattered them from there over all the earth, and they stopped building the city. 9 That is why it was called Babel—because there the Lord confused the language of the whole world. From there the Lord scattered them over the face of the whole earth. (Genesis 11:1-9)

1. Why did the people in Shinar want to build a tower reaching to the heavens? (Genesis 11:4)

2. Why did God stop them from completing their project? (Genesis 11:6)

3. How did God stop them from building the tower? (Genesis 11:7-9)

The word *Babel* sounds like the Hebrew word *Balal*, which means "confusion." God confused the people by creating different languages among them. Since they could only communicate with those who spoke the same language, the people were forced to move to different regions and live with those who spoke their language.

The list below describes the people of Shinar before God confused their language and after. Read over the list and answer the questions that follow.

<u>Before God Confused Their Language</u>	<u>After God Confused Their Language</u>
• United	• Divided
• Ambitious	• Discouraged
• Goal-oriented	• Confused
• Strong	• Weak

<table>
<tbody>
</tbody>
</table>

- Lived together
- Agreed on a plan
- Made progress on the tower

- Lived separately
- Cancelled their plan
- Stopped building the tower

Do you see how important communication was to the people in Shinar? Without a common, positive way to communicate, they couldn't accomplish their goals. In this example, God purposely thwarted the people's communication in order to carry out his plan.

However, in most cases, such as your relationship with your parents, God wants healthy, productive communication. If you or your parents cannot communicate effectively, neither of you will get your point across nor get what you want.

4. Is communication between you and your parents important to you? Why or why not?

5. On a scale of 1 to 10 (with 1 being a lot of fighting and negative communication, 5 being average communication, and 10 being very positive and open communication), how would you rate your communication with your parents? _____ Explain your answer.

Whether you rated communication with your parents a 1 or a 10, this week's lesson will be a valuable one for you. We'll discuss communication strategies to help both you and your parents.

Divorce is a stressful experience for everyone. But positive communication can make a difficult situation a little easier. Stick with the lessons this week, and you'll walk away with tools to help you both now and in the future.

DAY 2—THE DIFFICULTY OF COMMUNICATION

Yesterday we took a look at the story of the tower of Babel. We studied the importance of communication and what happens when we have poor or negative communication. So if communication is so important, why is it so difficult for you and your parents?

First of all, you're a part of two different generations. Maybe they want to understand your high-tech world, but after working, running errands, cleaning the house, and taking care of you (and your siblings, if you have any), keeping up with the latest gadgets just doesn't top their priority list.

Imagine if your parents moved the entire family to a new country. It would take time for you to learn what the teenagers in your new school considered cool, how they spoke, dressed, and acted. Your parents face this same challenge. They must learn an entirely new culture—the teen culture.

Second, communication is difficult because you're growing up. Your parents have invested years into molding you to be a responsible, likeable person. Maybe they're not yet ready to give up that control. They need to feel needed.

When a baby bird learns to fly, a momma bird leaves the nest to teach the baby the importance of flying. The momma also gives her baby bird some space to learn how to fly—and to fail, if necessary. Unfortunately, most human parents aren't so hands-off. Many parents want to keep their kids in the nest as long as possible. Your parents love you and want to protect you, but sometimes they don't know how to communicate this to you.

Third, communicating with parents is difficult because we live in a fast-paced world. You probably feel stretched to the limit between school, hockey practice, service club, youth group, a part-time job, and wanting to spend time with your friends. Your parents also have busy schedules: Working, raising a family, running errands, cooking dinner, cleaning the house, taking care of you and your siblings, not to mention trying to have a social life themselves. Your parents are tired by the end of the day.

Finally, communication is difficult because we all resist authority. Whether you like it or not, parents are authority figures in your life. You might not agree with their decisions or points of view, but they're in a position of authority over you and they don't need your approval. As long as your parents don't harm you physically, emotionally, or mentally, you need to abide by their rules.

Authority is a fact of life.

When you grow up and move out of your parents' house, you'll still live under someone's authority—a boss, our country's laws, and ultimately the authority of God.

Read Matthew 21:12-13 and answer the questions.

> Jesus entered the temple courts and drove out all who were buying and selling there. He overturned the tables of the money changers and the benches of those selling doves. "It is written," he said to them, " 'My house will be called a house of prayer,' but you are making it 'a den of robbers.' " (Matthew 21:12-13)

1. Why was Jesus angry with the money changers? Circle all that apply.

- They turned the sacred, holy temple into a place of business.
- They made a profit at the temple.
- They disrespected God in his own house.

You should've circled all the answers. But ultimately, the money changers' *greatest* sin was that they didn't respect God's authority. Their greed and selfishness drove them to seek profit instead of purification. God had created a sacred place for them to worship, and they trashed it.

When you disrespect your parents and defy their authority, they most likely become angry just like Jesus became angry with the money changers. And they'll be less inclined to work with you and give you what you want if they believe you don't respect them.

2. Do you respect your parents' authority?

3. If you answered no, explain why not.

4. If you answered yes, explain how this has helped you in a certain situation.

Today we looked at why communication is difficult for you and your parents. Tomorrow we'll look at communication tactics that don't work; in fact, they usually create more tension. We'll also look at healthy alternatives that will lead to harmony with your parents.

DAY 3—USING THE ROAD SIGNS

Yesterday we discussed why communication is so difficult for teenagers and their parents. Today we'll look at your current communication strategies and how you can improve your approach. Let's use the road signs to our advantage.

1. Look at this list of negative communication tactics and circle all that apply to you:

- Whining
- Nagging
- Slamming doors
- Hanging up the phone in the middle of a conversation
- Playing loud music in your room to avoid hearing your mom or dad talk to you
- Sassing, talking back
- Speaking with sarcasm
- Rolling your eyes
- Avoiding eye contact
- Yelling
- Manipulating to get what you want
- Choosing one parent over the other
- Giving the silent treatment

2. Think back to a time when you used one of these tactics with your parents. Describe the situation and the outcome.

Most likely, the outcome didn't play out in your favor. As we've already discovered, parents are overworked and underpaid. At the end of the day, they're tired. Their patience is short, and they don't respond well to whining, nagging, and so on. They just want your respect—just like you want their respect.

The next time you find yourself at a crossroads with your parents—you want to turn left, they want you to turn right—consider this list of alternate approaches.

- Instead of whining, sassing, talking back, speaking with sarcasm, yelling, or giving them the silent treatment…try speaking to your parents calmly and clearly.

- Instead of nagging…clearly explain to your parents what you want. Ask if you can agree on a date and time when they should reach a decision. For instance, if you want them to buy you a new baseball glove, let them know you need the glove before the big game on Saturday. Then ask if they can take you to the store on Tuesday. If that day doesn't work for them, what about Wednesday? By letting them know what you want, why you want it, and by when you want it, you shouldn't need to bug them about it more than once.

- Instead of slamming doors or playing loud music to drown out your parents…tell your parents you need a time out. Let them know you're frustrated (or angry or sad) and tell them you need 10 minutes to cool down. Then go hang out in your room for 10 minutes. Return to your mom or dad and finish the conversation when the 10 minutes are up. Chances are you'll both be in a better frame of mind.

- Instead of hanging up the phone in the middle of a conversation…ask your mom or dad if you can finish the discussion when you get home.

- Instead of rolling your eyes or avoiding eye contact…make eye contact with your parents. This shows you respect them and can handle an adult conversation. Rolling your eyes only shows them you're still immature in some ways. If they detect some immaturity, they're less likely to treat you with respect and give you what you want.

- Instead of manipulating them to get what you want…clearly outline what you want. Again, let them know what you want, why you want it, and by when you want it. Your parents will respect you when you clearly communicate your position.

- Instead of choosing one parent over the other…respect their individual rules. For example, let's say when you're at your mom's house she lets you hang out with your friends on a school night. But at your dad's house, school nights are reserved for homework. Don't use this against your dad. Instead, if your friends are hanging out on a school night, try negotiating with your dad. If you finish your homework, will he let you stay out until 9 p.m.? Show your dad that you're willing to keep your end of the bargain by completing your homework if he's willing to make an exception to the house rule. But if he refuses, you still need to respect him and his rules.

One thing that really frustrates parents is when they ask you, "What did you do at school today?" and you respond, "Nothing."

Your parents are genuinely interested in your classes, friends, and the challenges you face each day.

They want to know when you ace the big test so they can celebrate with you. They want to know when you're having trouble with your friends so they can offer advice or just listen.

But sometimes they want to talk when you don't. Some people don't like to talk in the car because they want to process the day. Some people don't like to talk while they're eating because they want to enjoy their meal and take time to unwind. I know many girls who enjoyed late-night chats while sitting in bed with their moms. Think about your day and consider when you're the most willing to open up to your parents. Circle all that apply.

- At the breakfast table
- On the way to school
- On the way home from school
- Before you start your homework
- Right after you finish your homework
- While your mom or dad is making dinner
- At the dinner table
- At night when you're getting ready to go to sleep

The next time your mom or dad dives into a conversation with you and you're not ready to talk, ask them if you can have some quiet time and pick up the conversation at the dinner table (or whatever time you think works best for you). Most likely they'll respect your space and look forward to talking with you later.

So what if you're good at communicating but your parents stink at it? What if your dad resorts to yelling or your mom immediately takes away privileges without talking to you about the situation? You can't control your parents' actions, but you can control how you react to them.

The best time to approach them is not in the heat of the discussion. If you think your parents are being unfair, let the dust settle before you approach them. After they've had time to cool down, let them know what you'd like to see changed. For instance, if your dad yelled at you, explain that his yelling makes you scared, upset, and uncomfortable. Ask him if you can talk about a way he can get his point across without yelling.

Don't forget the power of prayer. Pray that God would soften your parents' hearts. Pray they see your point of view, and that you understand their position as well. Pray for peace in your house. Matthew 5:9 states, "Blessed are the peacemakers, for they will be called children of God." God loves to see peace among his people, especially within families.

Communication is difficult for every family, especially those going through a divorce. But God can overcome all obstacles, including this one. Take some time today to commit to changing one negative way you communicate with your parents. Then ask God for the discipline and self-control to stick with this decision.

Dear God,

I want peace in my family. Please help me to stop _____
and instead _____

_____

_____

_____.

Please give my parents and me the patience to accomplish this. Help us glorify you through our relationship. Amen.

DAY 4—HANDLING CONFLICT

Like many of you, I experienced a house filled with yelling. My mom and stepfather had a dysfunctional, volatile relationship that resulted in angry screaming matches at all hours of the day and night. Yelling was the main form of communication in our house. In my mind, yelling was—and still is—explosive and scary. It taught me never to make waves for fear of the backlash that would follow.

As an adult, I've chosen the opposite reaction to conflict. Instead of yelling, I completely retreat and avoid talking about issues. Unfortunately, problems don't solve themselves. Instead they fester like a splinter in your finger, and they only get worse and more painful until I finally decide to deal with them. But by the time I address the issue, I feel so frustrated that I have a major meltdown and cry. My patient husband has learned my cycle of conflict resolution, and we're still figuring out how to handle conflict in a more positive way.

1. Describe how your parents communicate with you.

According to *The Unexpected Legacy of Divorce*, most children of divorce have difficulty dealing with communication and conflict because we didn't grow up in homes where positive communication existed.

Think about it this way: What if your parents never cleaned the house? They never emptied the trash, washed dishes, or put things away. Their stuff piled up until they couldn't avoid the clutter anymore. Then instead of cleaning, they chose to move to a new house and start the cycle all over again. If you grew up in a house like this, how would you ever know how to clean? You wouldn't know because your parents didn't teach you. If you live in a house filled with garbage, then chances are you'll think this is normal and also choose to live in a house filled with garbage when you're an adult.

The point of this chapter is for you to learn how to get rid of the garbage. Starting today you can begin throwing away those negative ways of dealing with conflict and replacing them with positive practices.

The *Unexpected Legacy of Divorce* lists the following ways in which children of divorce tend to solve conflict.[20]

2. Circle the one(s) that describes your typical reaction(s) to conflict.

- Hide your feelings
- Cry uncontrollably
- Become paralyzed and unable to work through the problem
- Retreat and ignore the problem
- Run away from the problem, no matter how small
- Respond with anger, yelling, and rebelling

Conflict is difficult in any family, but especially in divorced families. Aside from the normal parent-teenager conflict your friends experience (negotiating curfews, cell phone limits, Internet usage), you also must tackle some heavier issues, such as making time for each parent, taking on more responsibility around the house, and dealing with stepparents and stepsiblings. Instead of resorting to the things listed above, consider the following positive ways you can deal with conflict.

- **Talk.** Sounds simple, right? We all know talking about our feelings is difficult, especially when we don't think our parents will understand. Instead of yelling or stuffing your feelings, try talking about them with your parents. This needs to be a continuous conversation because your feelings will change daily according to the circumstances in your life.

Make an effort to keep your parents informed about how you're feeling.

For instance, if your dad wants to bring his new girlfriend to Thanksgiving dinner, explain to him that this idea makes you uncomfortable. Let him know that you want this day set aside for just the family. Try to reach a compromise. Maybe his girlfriend can come over at the end of the day for dessert instead. Or maybe you can all go to brunch the next day.

- **Listen.** Parents need to know that you respect them enough to listen to their side. You might have heard the old saying, "We have two ears and one mouth so that we can listen twice as much as we speak." Give your parents the opportunity to explain their position before you dive in and begin sharing your own.

- **Write them a letter.** In author Hayley DiMarco's book *Stupid Parents*, she advises teenagers to write letters to their parents.[21] If you have trouble verbally expressing your feelings, taking the time to write them down might help you express yourself more clearly. This works especially well in divorced families when you have an issue to tackle with both parents.

  For example, let's say your parents use you as their messenger to each other and you want them to stop. Getting them both in the same room long enough to explain your position could be a challenge. However, you can write them both a letter or email (letting them know you're sending the same letter to the other parent) and explain you no longer want to be put in the middle of their problems. When they see you take the time to put your feelings in writing, they'll pay attention. A letter or email also gives them something to look back on while they consider the issue.

- **Ask to schedule family meetings.** See if you can get one or both of your parents to agree to set aside a time each week to talk about the issues causing conflict in your family. Each week you can outline goals and expectations for the following week. When you come back the next week, you can talk about what you did to achieve these goals.

  Consider this: If your parents always nag you to do your chores, ask them to outline what chores need to be done on which day. Have them write it down (or you can write it down) and keep it somewhere visible, like posted on the refrigerator door. The following week you can both evaluate whether you met the goal of completing your chores on the assigned day. On the flip side, if you want your dad to stop coming home so late and missing dinner, ask him to make a pact with you that on three nights a week he'll come home by 6 p.m. At the following meeting, you'll know whether he kept this agreement.

- **Seek help from a family counselor.** If you use the positive communication techniques we discussed yesterday and you also try the above strategies for solving conflict and there's still tension in your family, ask your parents to seek family counseling. A trained, objective outsider can help both sides discover ways in which you can bring harmony into the family.

  Now take the time to pray about how you can improve the way you handle conflict. Write down your prayer.

DAY 5—CREATING HARMONY IN STEPFAMILIES

In today's culture, you probably have a friend whose parents divorced before your own. You most likely know you're not the only kid from a "broken home." But sometimes it feels like you're the only one struggling with the issues of divorce. Then, just when you're starting to get the hang of spending every other weekend with your dad and every other Christmas with your mom, one or both parents drops the bomb—they're getting remarried.

The latest national reports say 25 percent of all children will spend part of their childhood in a stepfamily.[22]

Obviously you're not alone. Millions of teenagers live in stepfamilies and face the same problems and issues you face. Today we'll look at ways we can avoid tension in stepfamilies and how we can use our newly found communication skills to diffuse fighting in the family.

1. If you have a stepparent, how do you feel about that person?

2. If your mom and dad aren't remarried, how do you feel about the possibility of remarriage?

Before you actually acquire a stepparent and stepsiblings, your mom and dad will begin dating. I know it might be gross to think about, but it's a fact. Many divorced parents start dating at the same time you start dating! Watching mom or dad date can be uncomfortable for some teenagers, so here are some boundaries you might want to talk about with your parents.

- Pick-Up Time—If your mom is dating, ask her if she's willing to meet her date at a public place. Let her know you're willing to meet someone she's dating after a reasonable amount of time, but you don't want to meet every man who picks her up for a date. This will prevent you from becoming emotionally attached to someone whom she may stop dating after a few weeks or months. This arrangement is also wise if you have negative feelings toward your mom dating, as you won't be forced into an awkward meeting before you're ready. This also allows her to keep some privacy in her life. If your dad is dating, chances are he'll go pick up his date, but run this idea by him, too, to make sure he understands your feelings.

- Reasonable Time Limit—After the initial first dates, your mom or dad might become seriously involved with someone. So when is the best time for you to meet this person? The answer is different for everyone. What seems reasonable to you? After three months of dating? Six months? You're walking a tightrope here—letting too much time pass means missing out on getting to know someone who could be your future stepparent. However, meeting someone too soon means setting yourself up for possible disappointment if the relationship doesn't work out. Decide on a reasonable time limit with your mom and dad and try to respect each other's needs on this issue.

- Holidays and Special Events—Many parents are excited about a new relationship and want to spend a great deal of time with their new love and include them in all events in their lives, including birthdays, holidays, and even your hockey games and gymnastics meets. If you're uncomfortable with your dad's girlfriend attending your hockey game, let your dad know. Ask him if you can all go out to dinner after the game instead of having her join in the activity. If you don't want your mom's boyfriend coming to the house on Christmas Day, ask your mom to compromise. Can he come over on Christmas Eve or for brunch the day after Christmas? Let her know you understand she wants to spend time with him, but you'd rather keep holidays reserved for family only.

    Of course, after a certain amount of time, your parents will insist on including their significant others at big events and you'll have to submit to their authority. But taking things slow in the beginning of a dating relationship is wise—even for your parents.

- TMI—Some parents have no filter, and they divulge too much information about their dating lives. If you're uncomfortable with the amount of details they share, let them know. I know you don't want to hurt their feelings, but having late-night chats with your dad about his love life is not appropriate. Being your parents' confidant is not your responsibility.

    Consider this statistic: Three-fourths of divorced men and two-thirds of divorced women remarry.[23] Chances are your mom will remarry, and there's an even greater likelihood your dad will remarry. Given these odds, let's look at a list of do's and don'ts that arise in stepfamilies.

Do Work Together on the Issue of Discipline

Two schools of thought exist on the issue of discipline in stepfamilies. Some believe only the biological parent, not the stepparent, should discipline the kids. Others believe the two adults are now a parental unit and should handle discipline together.

In the beginning of a new marriage, I believe only your mom or dad should handle the discipline. As time goes on, however, your stepparent will need to become part of the process. This is where those family meetings can be helpful. If your stepmom is upset that you leave your stuff all over the house, this issue can be brought to your attention with your dad in the same room. Then all three of you can reach a reasonable solution (which in this case would probably be that you need to stop leaving your stuff strewn all over the house).

I know it's tough to let someone who isn't your parent boss you around, but take into consideration that this is new territory for your stepparent, too. If your stepdad or stepmom doesn't have kids of their own, he or she might not understand what's "too strict." Work with your parent and your stepparent to make sure you're all on the same page.

Do Learn to Share

Along with a new stepparent, you might acquire stepsiblings. This can be a good experience or a difficult one. First, go into the relationship with an open mind. You might not like the same music or style of clothes, but you might enjoy the same movies. Take the time to get to know your new steps by having coffee, going for a walk, or just hanging out in your room.

Second, if your new stepsister moves into your house, don't be territorial. While sharing your television, phone, and bathroom might be difficult adjustments to make, she's probably having a hard time, too. Consider her position: She just moved into someone else's house, and now she has to abide by someone else's rules. She probably wants to figure out how to make this work as much as you do.

Do Stay Connected

If you live with your mom, she probably knows more about your day-to-day life than you want. But what about your dad? If you don't live with him, make the effort to stay connected. He misses being a part of your everyday life. He misses knowing what you did at school, what grade you made on your algebra test, and even what you ate for dinner. Keep him in the loop with emails and phone calls.

Do Ask Your Parents to Find a Common Ground

Hopefully your parents treat each other with respect after their divorce. However, parents who continue to fight post-divorce can make your life miserable. If they cannot attend your basketball game without fighting, then ask them to alternate attending games. However, events will arise when this arrangement won't be possible, such as graduation. Ahead of time, remind your parents that this is *your* day and ask them to try to keep their feelings about the other person at bay so you can all enjoy the day.

Don't Choose Sides

Some parents desperately want you to take sides. If your mom feels abandoned by your dad, she may fear you'll also abandon her. If your dad is angry with your mom, he might want you to be angry with her, too. Remember the saying "Misery loves company"? Sometimes moms and dads are so caught up in their own grief that they can't help but drag you down, too. But choosing sides is not your responsibility. Your parents divorced each other—not you.

Make it clear that you love them both and won't talk bad about either parent.

Don't Be a Mediator

Also, let your parents know you don't want to pass messages between them. If they need to communicate, then ask them to call or email each other. Keeping the lines of communication open between your parents is not your responsibility.

Don't Be a Sounding Board

We covered this earlier in regard to the issue of dating, but it applies to many areas in life. Your mom and dad shouldn't rely on you for venting all of their anger, frustration, and so on. If they tend to give you too much information, then let them know you're not comfortable with these discussions.

3. Which dos and don'ts seem easiest for you? Most difficult?

Communication is key to bringing harmony to your family and stepfamily. Although you cannot force everyone to get along, you can do your part. By treating your mom, dad, stepparent, and stepsiblings with respect—always asking, never demanding—you help set the tone for the family. Your parents will appreciate your effort and treat you with the same esteem.

Take a moment to ask God to help you use communication to improve your relationship with your parents, stepparents, and stepsiblings. Write down this prayer. And remember: God wants us to live in peace with one another.

GROUP SESSION
WEEK FOUR—DRIVER'S EDUCATION
How to Effectively Communicate with Your Parents

GOAL
This week help students find ways in which they can work together with their parents and stepparents during this time of change.

SUGGESTED ICEBREAKER
You'll need:
- A copy of "He Didn't Have to Be" (*Who Needs Pictures*, 1999)
- A CD player

Let the students listen to "He Didn't Have to Be" by Brad Paisley (*Who Needs Pictures*, 1999). You might want to find the lyrics online and print copies of them so the students can read the words of the song while they listen.

After the song ends, discuss the following questions:

1. What's the singer's attitude toward his stepfather?

2. If you have a stepparent, what's your attitude toward that person?

3. If you have stepparents and stepsiblings, do you generally get along with them?

4. What are some of the main issues that cause tension in your blended family?

5. If you could change one thing about your blended family, what would it be?

GROUP DISCUSSION
Ask the students to read the account of the tower of Babel in Genesis 11:1-9 and answer the following questions.

> 1 Now the whole world had one language and a common speech. 2 As people moved eastward, they found a plain in Shinar and settled there.
>
> 3 They said to each other, "Come, let's make bricks and bake them thoroughly." They used brick instead of stone, and tar for mortar. 4 Then they said, "Come, let us build ourselves

a city, with a tower that reaches to the heavens, so that we may make a name for ourselves and not be scattered over the face of the whole earth."

5 But the Lord came down to see the city and the tower that they were building. 6 The Lord said, "If as one people speaking the same language they have begun to do this, then nothing they plan to do will be impossible for them. 7 Come, let us go down and confuse their language so they will not understand each other."

8 So the Lord scattered them from there over all the earth, and they stopped building the city. 9 That is why it was called Babel—because there the Lord confused the language of the whole world. From there the Lord scattered them over the face of the whole earth. (Genesis 11:1-9)

1. Why was communication so important for the people of Shinar?

2. How is communication important in your relationship with your parents?

3. In your homework you read about some negative ways teenagers communicate with their parents. Which forms of communication do you use with your parents?

4. What's the outcome when you treat your parents this way?

5. How would you like to see this change?

. . . .

If your group meets for 12 weeks, wrap up the session after discussing negative ways in which they communicate with their parents and close simply in prayer and be open to any questions from your students. When you meet again in Week Eight, review these negative ways of communicating, and then explore healthy ways in which they can communicate with their parents noted on the forthcoming pages.

As an icebreaker for Week Eight, ask how they're feeling this week in general. Has anything happened in the past week that has stirred up strong emotions? Use this as a time to allow students to open up, encourage one another, and move to a deeper, more personal level of sharing.

Use the Closing Activity listed here as the Closing Activity for Week Eight.

Remind your students to read over their Week Seven (Chapter Four) homework on communication before you meet again.

. . . .

6. What are some healthy ways in which you can communicate with your parents? (Students should remember some of these were mentioned in their Week Four homework.)

- Speak to your parents calmly and clearly.

- Clearly explain to your parents what you want. Ask if you can agree on a date and time when they'll reach a decision.

- Take a time out when discussions with your parents get too heated.

- Make eye contact with your parents to show them you respect them and can handle an adult conversation.

- Don't play favorites with your parents.

- Don't manipulate your parents to get what you want.

- Avoid being the messenger. Ask your parents to communicate directly with one another—not through you.

- Write your parents a letter explaining your feelings.

- Ask for a family meeting time to discuss the issues that are on your mind.

- If all else fails, ask your parents to go with you to talk with a family counselor.

CLOSING ACTIVITY

Engage students in a role-playing exercise. Have them pair off and perform two skits for the group. One skit offers an example of poor communication while the other one offers an example of healthy communication.

- Skit #1: One student pretends to be the mom, and one plays the part of the son. Role-play a situation in which the mom refuses to allow her son to go camping with his dad because, according to the visitation schedule, it's her weekend with her son. The child reacts argumentatively and disrespectfully.

- Skit #2: Role-play the same situation as Skit #1, but this time the son reacts maturely and gives rational reasons for why his mom should let him go camping with his dad. The mom and son work out a compromise by the end of the skit.

TWO WRONGS DON'T MAKE A RIGHT

Choosing Forgiveness after a Divorce

Many people refuse to forgive someone for various reasons:

- Forgiveness excuses sin.
- Forgiveness gives a license to sin.
- Forgiveness is a sign of weakness.
- He'll think he didn't hurt me.
- She'll think she can do it again.
- He won't have to deal with the consequences of his actions.
- She doesn't deserve my forgiveness.
- Not forgiving him is my way of punishing him.
- Not forgiving her will teach her a lesson.

All of these thoughts and feelings are valid, but they aren't true. The truth is, forgiveness doesn't erase someone's sin. Forgiveness doesn't lessen the person's offense. Forgiveness only sets free the hurt person—free of anger, free of sadness.

This week we'll look at the power of forgiveness and how it can set us free when our parents divorce.

DAY 1—THE ROAD LESS TRAVELED

My brother, who's four years older than me, loved to torment me when we were kids. (It's hard to believe an older brother would terrorize his little sister, right?) But when I'd retaliate with whining, crying, or tattling, my grandma always responded, "Two wrongs don't make a right."

Grandma was trying to teach me that I needed to find a different approach to dealing with my brother. After all, he was older, smarter, and stronger than I was. I obviously couldn't beat him at his own game, but I could choose to forgive and move on. This was hard to do when he cut my doll's hair into a Mohawk or gave me a wedgie in front of his friends. But no matter how small or large the offense, my grandma wanted me to forgive him. She understood that if I forgave my brother enough times, he'd eventually get bored and leave me alone. Grandma talked with my brother about protecting and loving me, his younger sister. Yet she also taught me that I needed to take a different approach in dealing with my big brother. After all, he wasn't trying to be mean—he was only trying to show his little sister who was "in charge."

Although my brother has stopped giving me wedgies, there are still times in life when I'm faced with the choice to forgive someone or harbor anger and resentment against that person. Divorce offers many opportunities to practice our forgiveness skills, so let's look at God's Word to find out what God says about forgiveness.

Over the next two days we'll study the story of Joseph. This young man has much to teach us about the power of forgiveness and how we can apply this to our parents' divorce.

Pause for a moment to read the incredible story of Joseph in Genesis 37:2-36 and Genesis 39:1–47:28. Then answer the following questions.

1. Describe, in your own words, why Joseph's brothers sold him into slavery. (Genesis 37:2-11)

This is the account of Jacob's family line.

Joseph, a young man of seventeen, was tending the flocks with his brothers, the sons of Bilhah and the sons of Zilpah, his father's wives, and he brought their father a bad report about them.

Now Israel loved Joseph more than any of his other sons, because he had been born to him in his old age; and he made a richly ornamented robe for him. When his brothers saw that their father loved him more than any of them, they hated him and could not speak a kind word to him.

Joseph had a dream, and when he told it to his brothers, they hated him all the more. He said to them, "Listen to this dream I had: We were binding sheaves of grain out in the field when suddenly my sheaf rose and stood upright, while your sheaves gathered around mine and bowed down to it."

His brothers said to him, "Do you intend to reign over us? Will you actually rule us?" And they hated him all the more because of his dream and what he had said.

Then he had another dream, and he told it to his brothers. "Listen," he said, "I had another dream, and this time the sun and moon and eleven stars were bowing down to me."

When he told his father as well as his brothers, his father rebuked him and said, "What is this dream you had? Will your mother and I and your brothers actually come and bow down to the ground before you?" His brothers were jealous of him, but his father kept the matter in mind. (Genesis 37:2-11)

2. Instead of killing him, Joseph's brothers sold him to the Ishmaelites. As Joseph's new owners drove him away from his family and the only home he'd ever known, how do you think he felt? What thoughts might have swirled through his mind?

While Joseph was enslaved in Potiphar's house, Potiphar's wife falsely accused Joseph of a crime (Genesis 39:1-20). Even though the authorities threw Joseph into prison, God never left him.

Now Joseph had been taken down to Egypt. Potiphar, an Egyptian who was one of Pharaoh's officials, the captain of the guard, bought him from the Ishmaelites who had taken him there.

The Lord was with Joseph so that he prospered, and he lived in the house of his Egyptian Master. When his master saw that the Lord was with him and that the Lord gave him success in everything he did, Joseph found favor in his eyes and became his attendant. Potiphar put him in charge of his household, and he entrusted to his care everything he owned. From the time he put him in charge of his household and of all that he owned, the Lord blessed the household of the Egyptian because of Joseph. The blessing of the Lord was on everything Potiphar had, both in the house and in the field. So Potiphar left everything he had in Joseph's care; with Joseph in charge, he did not concern himself with anything except the food he ate.

Now Joseph was well-built and handsome, and after a while his master's wife took notice of Joseph and said, "Come to bed with me!"

But he refused. "With me in charge," he told her, "my master does not concern himself with anything in the house; everything he owns he has entrusted to my care. No one is greater in this house than I am. My master has withheld nothing from me except you, because you are his wife. How then could I do such a wicked thing and sin against God?" And though she spoke to Joseph day after day, he refused to go to bed with her or even be with her.

One day he went into the house to attend to his duties, and none of the household servants was inside. She caught him by his cloak and said, "Come to bed with me!" But he left his cloak in her hand and ran out of the house.

When she saw that he had left his cloak in her hand and had run out of the house, she called her household servants. "Look," she said to them, "this Hebrew has been brought to us to make sport of us! He came in here to sleep with me, but I screamed. When he heard me scream for help, he left his cloak beside me and ran out of the house."

She kept his cloak beside her until his master came home. Then she told him this story: "That Hebrew slave you brought us came to me to make sport of me. But as soon as I screamed for help, he left his cloak beside me and ran out of the house."

When his master heard the story his wife told him, saying, "This is how your slave treated me," he burned with anger. Joseph's master took him and put him in prison, the place where the king's prisoners were confined. (Genesis 39:1-20)

3. As Joseph sat in his cold, wet, jail cell, what thoughts and feelings do you think he experienced? Check all that apply:

❑ Anger
❑ Bitterness
❑ Sadness
❑ Fear
❑ Isolation
❑ Hatred
❑ Trust
❑ Faith
❑ Love
❑ Hope
❑ Joy
❑ Other: _____

Now, circle each feeling that relates to how you feel about your parents' divorce.

4. How did God protect Joseph in an unfair and difficult situation? (Genesis 39:20-23)

But while Joseph was there in the prison, the Lord was with him; he showed him kindness and granted him favor in the eyes of the prison warden. So the warden put Joseph in charge of all those held in the prison, and he was made responsible for all that was done there. The warden paid no attention to anything under Joseph's care, because the Lord was with Joseph and gave him success in whatever he did. (Genesis 39:20-23)

So how does Joseph's story relate to divorce? When Joseph's brothers sold him into slavery, they did so without his consent or input. I'm confident Joseph would not have chosen to leave his family, friends, and home to go work as a slave in a foreign land. In many ways his plight parallels your parents' divorce. You didn't choose it, yet you must deal with the aftermath. You, like Joseph, may have left your family, friends, and home to start a new life somewhere else. If so, then you can probably identify with Joseph's feelings as he drove away with the Ishmaelites and watched his life disappear in the dust.

But I want you to realize that just as God protected Joseph, he also protects you and me amidst our trials. I've seen God's provision during one of the most challenging times of my life. As I said before, I attended three different high schools in three different cities after my mom's second divorce. I experienced fear, sadness, doubt, anger, bitterness, and resentment during those times of transition. Yet God continued to care for me by always surrounding me with godly friends and positive activities. Without the support of these organizations and the people involved, I would have drowned in my loneliness.

Take some time to examine your own life since your parents' divorce. We already discussed changes that occur after divorce, but today I want you to think about how God cares for you in the middle of those changes.

5. How has God provided for you since your parents' divorce? Check all that apply:

❑ Friends with whom I can talk about my parents' divorce
❑ Family members who look out for me
❑ Christian support through youth group, church, or other organizations
❑ School activities that use my gifts and talents
❑ A part-time job
❑ A sense of peace and forgiveness
❑ Strength to get through the most difficult days
❑ Ways to communicate with my parents
❑ Other:

Rest assured: God is with you.

God also provided this Bible study to help you work through your thoughts and feelings. God longs for you to find healing and forgiveness in this difficult situation. As I write this, I'm praying that as you stand at these crossroads, you'll choose Christ. I pray you won't bury yourself in sadness, anger, and hopelessness, but that you'll seek comfort and joy in Christ.

Take some time now to thank God for his provision during this time in your life. If you have trouble seeing God's presence in your life, pray for God to reveal himself to you. Pray

God will show you how he's actively involved in your life. Write down this prayer.

DAY 2—THE ROAD LESS TRAVELED (CONTINUED)

Yesterday you read the story of Joseph, a young Hebrew boy sold into slavery by his brothers. Joseph experienced many trials, yet God remained present and active in his life. Joseph trusted in God's plan throughout the difficult times, and his faith allowed him to see the big picture and extend forgiveness to his brothers.

Today we'll finish studying Joseph's life and look at how God rewarded Joseph's unfailing faith. As you read through the questions and Scripture today, let's remember that the account of Joseph's life isn't merely a story; he's a real person who lived thousands of years ago. Yet despite the lapse in time, we can still identify with his hardships and learn from his powerful example of forgiveness. Let's begin our study.

While imprisoned, Joseph warned Pharaoh that a famine would destroy Egypt if they didn't take action. Joseph devised a plan, and Pharaoh elevated him to a high position so he could execute this plan.

1. In Genesis 41:57 we learn that the famine affected not only Egypt, but also _____. This included Joseph's family living in the land of Canaan.

> And all the world came to Egypt to buy grain from Joseph, because the famine was severe everywhere. (Genesis 41:57).

2. Why did Joseph's brothers travel to Egypt? (Genesis 42:1-5)

> When Jacob learned that there was grain in Egypt, he said to his sons, "Why do you just keep looking at each other?" He continued, "I have heard that there is grain in Egypt. Go down there and buy some for us, so that we may live and not die."
>
> Then ten of Joseph's brothers went down to buy grain from Egypt. But Jacob did not send Benjamin, Joseph's brother, with the others, because he was afraid that harm might come to him. So Israel's sons were among those who went to buy grain, for the famine was in the land of Canaan also. (Genesis 42:1-5)

3. When his brothers came to Egypt, Joseph identified them immediately; but his brothers didn't recognize Joseph. Why do you think they didn't know they were speaking to Joseph? (Genesis 42:6-13)

Now Joseph was the governor of the land, the person who sold grain to all its people. So when Joseph's brothers arrived, they bowed down to him with their faces to the ground. As soon as Joseph saw his brothers, he recognized them, but he pretended to be a stranger and spoke harshly to them. "Where do you come from?" he asked. "From the land of Canaan," they replied, "to buy food."

Although Joseph recognized his brothers, they did not recognize him. Then he remembered his dreams about them and said to them, "You are spies! You have come to see where our land is unprotected."

"No, my lord," they answered. "Your servants have come to buy food. We are all the sons of one man. Your servants are honest men, not spies."

"No!" he said to them. "You have come to see where our land is unprotected."

But they replied, "Your servants were twelve brothers, the sons of one man, who lives in the land of Canaan. The youngest is now with our father, and one is no more." (Genesis 42:6-13)

The Bible doesn't tell us why Joseph's brothers didn't recognize him, but we can speculate a few possible answers:

- They believed Joseph would have died by this time because a slave's life was so difficult.
- They'd know a former slave would never serve in such a prestigious position.
- Joseph had matured physically and emotionally due to the trials he'd endured.

4. When Joseph finally revealed his identity to his brothers, how did they respond according to Genesis 45:3? Check the box that applies:

❑ They wept.
❑ They became angry.
❑ They stood speechless.
❑ They ran away.

Joseph said to his brothers, "I am Joseph! Is my father still living?" But his brothers were not able to answer him, because they were terrified at his presence. (Genesis 45:3)

• Why did they respond this way?

❏ They felt sad.
❏ They felt terrified.
❏ They felt ashamed.

Joseph extended grace and forgiveness to his brothers despite their betrayal. Read Genesis 45:4-8 and answer the following questions.

Then Joseph said to his brothers, "Come close to me." When they had done so, he said, "I am your brother Joseph, the one you sold into Egypt! And now, do not be distressed and do not be angry with yourselves for selling me here, because it was to save lives that God sent me ahead of you. For two years now there has been famine in the land, and for the next five years there will be no plowing and reaping. But God sent me ahead of you to preserve for you a remnant on earth and to save your lives by a great deliverance.

So then, it was not you who sent me here, but God. He made me father to Pharaoh, lord of his entire household and ruler of all Egypt." (Genesis 45:4-8)

5. Joseph told his brothers not to be _____ and _____ with themselves.

This act of love takes incredible humility and forgiveness. Believe me, if my brother sold me into slavery (as I'm sure he wanted to when we were kids), then I'd certainly want him to feel guilty! But Joseph recognized the bigger picture.

6. Joseph didn't hold his brothers responsible for sending him to Egypt—despite the fact that they'd handed him over to the Midianite merchants. Who does Joseph believe brought him to Egypt?

7. Joseph recognizes not only who sent him to Egypt, but also why. Read Genesis 50:20. For what reason does Joseph believe he was sent to Egypt?

"You intended to harm me, but God intended it for good to accomplish what is now being done, the saving of many lives." (Genesis 50:20)

Joseph displays humility, maturity, grace, love, and forgiveness. His position in the Egyptian kingdom gave him the right to punish his brothers—even to kill them—for their act of betrayal. Yet Joseph chose the road less traveled. He chose to forgive them. He also took the opportunity to show them God's providence. What an awesome witness he is to God's plan for our lives.

8. Has someone hurt you? If so, write about it here.

9. How can you apply Joseph's situation to your own life?

10. Now, take some time to consider how God might use this hurt to glorify himself.

If you cannot think of any way in which this betrayal or loss will work out for good, ask God to show you his plan for you. Remember, Joseph endured years of hardship before God's plan came to fruition. God might not reveal his plan for us for days, weeks, months, or years, even though we want instant answers. In the meantime, rest in God's promise that he works out all things in order to glorify himself and to bless his children. Romans 8:28 promises us "that in all things God works for the good of those who love him, who have been called according to his purpose."

Joseph's grace, mercy, and forgiveness toward his brothers are an amazing reflection of God's grace toward us. If you're holding on to any anger or bitterness toward your mom or dad for their divorce (or for any other reasons), ask God to help you release that bitterness. Pray for a heart of forgiveness. Write down this prayer.

DAY 3—NOT EVEN A SCRATCH

As a new driver, you might have experienced a few fender benders. I've sure had my share of tickets and accidents, so I won't cast the first stone. Sometimes I claimed responsibility for an accident; other times the other driver was at fault. Either way, I've paid thousands of dollars for damage done to several of my cars over the years—not a fun way to spend money.

One day, after parking in a crowded parking lot, I opened my car door, and it lightly tapped the car next to me. I stepped out of my car and checked the other car to make sure I hadn't caused any damage. Little did I know, the car's owner saw the incident and watched my inspection. When I looked up and realized he was standing near me, I sheepishly smiled and said, "I'm so sorry. But it looks like there isn't even a scratch on your door." Fortunately, the man said, "Oh, no problem," and proceeded to get in his car and drive away.

Phew! That could have been a sticky situation. But this man's instant forgiveness and grace prevented the situation from escalating.

God wants his children to respond just as this man did—extend forgiveness to someone who wrongs us. For the next two days, we'll study the parable of the unmerciful servant. Take the time right now to read Matthew 18:23-35.

[Jesus said:] "Therefore, the kingdom of heaven is like a king who wanted to settle accounts with his servants. As he began the settlement, a man who owed him ten thousand bags of gold was brought to him. Since he was not able to pay, the master ordered that he and his wife and his children and all that he had be sold to repay the debt.

"The servant fell on his knees before him. 'Be patient with me,' he begged, 'and I will pay back everything.' The servant's master took pity on him, canceled the debt and let him go.

"But when that servant went out, he found one of his fellow servants who owed him a hundred silver coins. He grabbed him and began to choke him. 'Pay back what you owe me!' he demanded.

"His fellow servant fell to his knees and begged him, 'Be patient with me, and I will pay you back.'

"But he refused. Instead, he went off and had the man thrown into prison until he could pay the debt. When the other servants saw what had happened, they were greatly distressed and went and told their master everything that had happened.

"Then the master called the servant in. 'You wicked servant,' he said, 'I canceled all that debt of yours because you begged me to. Shouldn't you have had mercy on your fellow servant just as I had on you?' In anger his master handed him over to the jailers to be tortured, until he should pay back all he owed.

"This is how my heavenly Father will treat each of you unless you forgive a brother or sister from your heart." (Matthew 18:23-35)

Jesus used parables to convey truth to people. He said not everyone who heard would understand. Therefore, he used symbolism so only those seeking God's wisdom would truly understand his message.

Let's look at the symbolism of this parable.

1. What does the debt represent?

2. Who does the king represent?

3. Who does the unmerciful servant represent?

Note that the unmerciful servant owed the king 10,000 gold bags (or talents)—a huge sum of money! Meanwhile, the second servant owed the unmerciful servant only a hundred silver coins.

4. Why are these amounts so significant?

The amount the first servant owed was so large he'd never be capable of repaying it. Yet, when a fellow servant owed an amount insignificant by comparison, the first servant offered no grace or understanding. He responded with anger and wrath.

5. How does this parable relate to our own sin?

6. According to this parable, how should we treat others when they sin against us?

7. According to Matthew 18:32-35, how will God treat us if we don't forgive others?

This parable is straightforward about our need to forgive others. Tomorrow we'll continue to use this parable to discuss how we can forgive those who've hurt us.

Feel free to close by praying the following words: "Lord, please examine my heart. Reveal to me any lack of forgiveness I'm carrying with me. Help me forgive those who've hurt or disappointed me. Reveal to me also people I need forgiveness from for any wrong I may have done. Help me to live with a merciful heart. Amen."

DAY 4—NOT EVEN A SCRATCH (CONTINUED)

Yesterday we studied the parable of the unmerciful servant. Today we'll continue looking at this passage. Take a moment to review Matthew 18:23-35. Then answer the questions below.

1. Reflect on your own life for a moment. Have you ever received forgiveness like the master extended to his servant? Explain here.

During my sophomore year in college, I lived with four girls in a two-bedroom apartment. We had enough hairdryers and curling irons to open a small hair salon! The year was filled with many highs and lows, and while making plans for the next year, three of us decided to live together during our junior year—without the other two roommates. This caused many hurt feelings.

I'd been a friend to one of these left-out roommates since the seventh grade. And although I knew I'd hurt her deeply, I didn't realize the impact this decision had made on her mom. This mother watched her daughter struggle through the situation; and as a result, she became very angry with me. Only years later did my friend's mom confess her anger and extend her forgiveness to me.

In this situation, I was the first servant, receiving mercy and forgiveness from the king. I'd committed a sin I couldn't possibly repay, yet she forgave me. My friend, her mom, and I all became extremely close after that experience. But this close relationship wouldn't have been possible if her mom hadn't forgiven me.

2. Have you ever extended forgiveness to someone? Explain.

3. Have you ever refused to forgive someone? Explain.

Take a moment right now to ask God to help you forgive that person.

4. God is clear about how often we should forgive others. Read Matthew 18:21-22. How many times should we forgive someone?

> Then Peter came to Jesus and asked, "Lord, how many times shall I forgive someone who sins against me? Up to seven times?"
>
> Jesus answered, "I tell you, not seven times, but [seventy times seven]." (Matthew 18:21-22)

5. What does "seventy times seven" mean? Does it mean we should forgive someone 490 times and then stop forgiving them?

Jesus uses hyperbole (an exaggeration) to make a point. He clearly wants us to forgive others no matter how many times they sin against us.

Forgiveness is an important tool in recovering from our parents' divorce. Have you forgiven your parents for the parts they played in the divorce?

Yes   No

If you've forgiven your parents, pray that God would continue to help you forgive them as new challenges arise. If haven't forgiven your parents, ask God to give you a heart of compassion and forgiveness for your parents. Write down this prayer.

DAY 5—CRUISE CONTROL

We devoted this past week to the topic of forgiveness and how it relates to our parents' divorce. The theme of forgiveness weaves through the Bible in the lives of many people, yet it's sometimes difficult for us to carry it out in our own lives. Why? Because we buy into many lies and misconceptions about forgiveness.

At the beginning of the week, you read a list of reasons why we avoid forgiving someone who's hurt us. Read the list again and check the box if the statement applies to your thoughts on forgiveness.

❑ Forgiveness excuses sin.
❑ Forgiveness gives a license to sin.
❑ Forgiveness is a sign of weakness.
❑ He'll think he didn't hurt me.
❑ She'll think she can do it again.
❑ He won't have to deal with the consequences of his actions.
❑ She doesn't deserve my forgiveness.
❑ Not forgiving him is my way of punishing him.
❑ Not forgiving her will teach her a lesson.

Those statements might describe your thoughts and feelings about forgiveness, but they're Satan's lies. He wants us to stay trapped in our anger and bitterness because we're unable to grow closer to Christ if we're unable to love and forgive others. Our separation from Christ is exactly what Satan wants.

Read the following verses in order to understand God's truth about forgiveness. As you study these verses and answer the questions, think about how they relate to your parents' divorce.

1. Why should we forgive other people? (Ephesians 4:32)

Be kind and compassionate to one another, forgiving each other, just as in Christ God forgave you. (Ephesians 4:32)

2. What role does Jesus play in our forgiveness? (1 John 2:2)

He is the atoning sacrifice for our sins, and not only for ours but also for the sins of the whole world. (1 John 2:2)

3. What must we do before receiving God's forgiveness? (Matthew 6:14-15)

"For if you forgive others when they sin against you, your heavenly Father will also forgive you. But if you do not forgive others their sins, your Father will not forgive your sins." (Matthew 6:14-15)

4. What must we do in order to forgive others? (Luke 7:44-47)

Then he turned toward the woman and said to Simon, "Do you see this woman? I came into your house. You did not give me any water for my feet, but she wet my feet with her tears and wiped them with her hair. You did not give me a kiss, but this woman, from the time I entered, has not stopped kissing my feet. You did not put oil on my head, but she has poured perfume on my feet. Therefore, I tell you, her many sins have been forgiven—as her great love has shown. But whoever has been forgiven little loves little." (Luke 7:44-47)

The main point I want to stress is that God calls us to forgive others, including our parents, for one reason only: Because God forgave us. And God continues to forgive us daily. If the perfect Creator of the earth can extend forgiveness, shouldn't we also extend forgiveness to those around us? Or are we above that?

I also want you to grasp the depth of God's forgiveness by reading the verses above. Do you know you can have eternal life because of God's forgiveness? You have the power to forgive others because Jesus Christ forgave those who sinned against him.

> *Jesus said, "Father, forgive them, for they do not know what they are doing."*
> *(Luke 23:34)*

If you've never received Christ's forgiveness, I want you to take a moment and think about this decision. You're standing at a crossroads—the choice is yours. Sure, you can continue to wander through life, just driving with the cruise control turned on and thinking you're completely independent and in control. But believe me when I say you'll eventually crash.

Or you can surrender your life, your worries, your fears, and your control to a heavenly Father who created you and loves you. You can accept how God's sovereignty brought you to this point in your life and embrace God's offer of an abundant life on earth and an eternal life in heaven. If you're ready to give your life to God, pray this prayer right now:

Jesus,

Thank you for your sacrifice. Thank you for giving your life so I can have eternal life. Please forgive me for all of the sinful thoughts and actions I commit daily. I admit I need a Savior. I cannot live this life alone. I pray you'll take control of my heart and mind. Make me a new creation in your image. I confess you're my Lord and Savior. There is none like you. Amen.

That's our closing prayer today. If you just prayed this prayer for the first time, please talk to someone about it—a trusted friend or family member, a counselor, or your youth pastor. Tell someone about your decision to accept Christ and ask that person to pray for you during this exciting time in your life.

If you've already accepted Christ as your Savior, take a moment to pray for those still struggling with the decision. Pray they wouldn't ignore God's call but would surrender their lives to the King.

GROUP SESSION
WEEK FIVE—TWO WRONGS DON'T MAKE A RIGHT
Choosing Forgiveness after a Divorce

GOAL
This week we'll define *forgiveness* according to the Bible and discuss areas in which we need to forgive others.

SUGGESTED ICEBREAKER
You'll need:
• A copy of "Prodigal Dad" (*Out of My Mind*, 2001)
• A CD player"

Let the students listen to "Prodigal Dad" by GS Megaphone (*Out of My Mind*, 2001). You might want to find the lyrics online and print copies of them so the students can read the words of the song while they listen.

After the song ends, discuss the following questions:

1. Describe the singer's feelings when his dad leaves.

2. Can you identify with any of these feelings?

3. Who fills the void left by the singer's dad?

4. Why was the singer able to forgive his dad?

GROUP DISCUSSION
This past week the students studied three biblical examples of forgiveness: Joseph, the unmerciful servant, and Jesus Christ. Today you'll discuss the students' reactions to these people. This week's lesson is crucial because it not only challenges the students to forgive others, but it also invites them to accept Christ's forgiveness.

The Story of Joseph
Begin by recapping the story of Joseph's life (Genesis 37:2-36 and 39:1–47:28) and include the following highlights:

• Joseph saw God's providence during a difficult situation. (Genesis 45:3-8)

• Joseph forgave his brothers through his actions and words. (Genesis 47:11-12; 50:19-21)

Ask:

1. Do you see God's providence in your own life? Explain.

2. How has God turned a difficult situation into a blessing in your life?

3. How does forgiveness benefit the person offering the forgiveness?

4. How does forgiveness benefit the person receiving the forgiveness?

Parable of the Unmerciful Servant

Summarize this parable (Matthew 18:23-35). Then ask the students to answer the questions that follow.

[Jesus said:] "Therefore, the kingdom of heaven is like a king who wanted to settle accounts with his servants. As he began the settlement, a man who owed him ten thousand bags of gold was brought to him. Since he was not able to pay, the master ordered that he and his wife and his children and all that he had be sold to repay the debt.

"The servant fell on his knees before him. 'Be patient with me,' he begged, 'and I will pay back everything.' The servant's master took pity on him, canceled the debt and let him go.

"But when that servant went out, he found one of his fellow servants who owed him a hundred silver coins. He grabbed him and began to choke him. 'Pay back what you owe me!' he demanded.

"His fellow servant fell to his knees and begged him, 'Be patient with me, and I will pay you back.'

"But he refused. Instead, he went off and had the man thrown into prison until he could pay the debt. When the other servants saw what had happened, they were greatly distressed and went and told their master everything that had happened.

"Then the master called the servant in. 'You wicked servant,' he said, 'I canceled all that debt of yours because you begged me to. Shouldn't you have had mercy on your fellow servant just as I had on you?' In anger his master handed him over to the jailers to be tortured, until he should pay back all he owed.

"This is how my heavenly Father will treat each of you unless you forgive a brother or sister from your heart." (Matthew 18:23-35)

Ask:

1. Who does the king represent?

2. Who does the unmerciful servant represent?

3. What does the debt represent?

4. What's significant about the amounts of money?

5. Jesus says we should forgive someone "seventy times seven" (Matthew 18:22). Should we take this number literally? What does Jesus mean here?

6. What's the main point Jesus teaches through this parable?

7. How can you apply this to your life? To your parents' divorce?

. . . .

If your group meets for 12 weeks, wrap up the session after discussing the parable of the unmerciful servant and close simply in prayer and be open to any questions from your students. When you meet again in Week 10, review the subject of forgiveness and what you discussed from Week Nine. Then discuss Jesus Christ as the ultimate example of forgiveness.

As an icebreaker for Week 10, ask how they're feeling this week in general. Has anything happened in the past week that has stirred up strong emotions? Use this as a time to allow students to open up, encourage one another, and move to a deeper, more personal level of sharing.

Use the Closing Activity listed here as the Closing Activity for Week 10.

Remind your students to read over their Week Nine (Chapter Five) homework on forgiveness before you meet again.

. . . .

Jesus Christ

Discuss the misconceptions about forgiveness listed here and in the Student Guide. Ask them which ideas they believe and why. Then continue the discussion with the questions that follow.

- Forgiveness excuses sin.
- Forgiveness gives a license to sin.

- Forgiveness is a sign of weakness.
- He'll think he didn't hurt me.
- She'll think she can do it again.
- He won't have to deal with the consequences of his actions.
- She doesn't deserve my forgiveness.
- Not forgiving him is my way of punishing him.
- Not forgiving her will teach her a lesson.

1. Ask one of your students to read Romans 6:1-2. How does this verse expose the lie that forgiveness gives someone a license to sin?

What shall we say, then? Shall we go on sinning so that grace may increase? By no means! We are those who have died to sin; how can we live in it any longer? (Romans 6:1-2)

2. Ask another student to read Romans 12:19. What does this verse say about revenge?

Do not take revenge, my dear friends, but leave room for God's wrath, for it is written: "It is mine to avenge; I will repay," says the Lord. (Romans 12:19)

3. Is it difficult for you to forgive others? Why or why not?

4. Why does God want us to forgive others?

Take this opportunity to share the gospel with your students, stressing our need as sinful people to receive Christ's forgiveness. Let your students know they cannot fully forgive their parents if they haven't received the cleansing forgiveness of Jesus Christ. Let your students know that if any of them would like to accept Christ as their Lord and Savior, they can do so right now or talk with you privately after the group discussion ends.

CLOSING ACTIVITY

Play another clip from *A Walk to Remember*. This clip begins when Landon (played by Shane West) goes to visit Jamie (played by Mandy Moore) in the hospital. Jamie's dad (played by Peter Coyote) shares that Landon's dad has agreed to pay for Jamie's home health care. Continue playing the clip through the scene

YOU'LL NEED—
- A copy of *A Walk to Remember* (Warner Bros., 2002), cued to 1:28:04 and end clip at 1:29:26.
- A television or video projection unit
- A DVD player
- Notepaper
- Pencils

where Landon visits his dad and offers his thanks and forgiveness. Then ask students the following questions.

1. Why do you think Landon forgave his dad?

2. Was Landon forgiving his dad for not helping Jamie in the beginning? Or was Landon forgiving his dad for more than that? Explain.

3. Landon needed to lay down his pride and take up humility in order to forgive his dad. How hard do you think this was for him? Explain.

4. Are you willing to offer this same kind of forgiveness to your parents?

Now distribute paper and pencils to the students. Ask them to write letters to their parents offering them forgiveness for anything that still needs resolution and healing regarding the divorce. Are they angry with their moms? Do they blame their dads?

Also, ask the students if there's anything for which they need to ask their parents' forgiveness—words they wish they could take back; a situation handled poorly. Whatever the circumstance, encourage the students to open the lines of communication with these letters.

If the students aren't emotionally ready to do this, then instead ask them to write letters to God and talking to God about why they're not ready to forgive their parents. In this letter they should ask God to work in their hearts so they can eventually forgive their parents.

THE END OF THE ROAD

Growing Closer to Christ

You made it! You've reached the last week of our study. I pray the last five weeks have given you the chance to work through some of those difficult thoughts and feelings about divorce that maybe you hadn't considered. I also pray that you're grasping the depth of God's love for you. This week we'll discuss how we can grow closer to Christ during a trial like divorce.

DAY 1—A BUMP IN THE ROAD

Have you ever been driving down the road when suddenly—BUMP!—the car bounces up and then pounds down on the ground? Then the car starts to shake as you slow down and cautiously pull over to the side of the road. When you step out and walk around the car to investigate the problem, you realize you just drove over a spike, and it punctured a hole in your front right tire.

Unfortunately, you then realize you forgot to put the spare tire back in the trunk after you cleaned out the car last week. Now you must pay for a new tire *and* a tow truck.

This little mishap causes you to miss soccer practice. So the coach benches you for the next three games. Now your dad is furious with you for behaving irresponsibly, and he grounds you from driving the car for a month.

As if things couldn't get any worse, that same week your mom calls to say she can't attend this year's sports banquet. Your girlfriend (or boyfriend) breaks up with you, you fail your chemistry test, and your friends plan a camping trip without you. Nothing seems to be working out for you lately.

Does this sound familiar? If so, then you can identify with Job. God described Job as "blameless and upright" (Job 1:1, 8). Yet despite his faith and righteousness, Job suffered many trials. For the next two days, we'll learn about Job's life and how these trials brought him closer to God instead of driving a wedge between them.

Take a few minutes to read Job 1–2, and then answer the questions below:

1. According to Job 1:1, what kind of man was Job? <u>Blameless</u> and <u>upright</u>.

In the land of Uz there lived a man whose name was Job. This man was blameless and upright; he feared God and shunned evil. (Job 1:1)

2. How was Job a blessed man? (Job 1:2-3)

He had seven sons and three daughters, and he owned seven thousand sheep, three thousand camels, five hundred yoke of oxen and five hundred donkeys, and had a large number of servants. He was the greatest man among all the people of the East. (Job 1:2-3)

3. Why did Satan want to attack Job (Job 1:6-12)?

One day the angels came to present themselves before the Lord, and Satan also came with them. The Lord said to Satan, "Where have you come from?"

Satan answered the Lord, "From roaming through the earth and going back and forth in it."

Then the Lord said to Satan, "Have you considered my servant Job? There is no one on earth like him; he is blameless and upright, a man who fears God and shuns evil."

"Does Job fear God for nothing?" Satan replied. "Have you not put a hedge around him and his household and everything he has? You have blessed the work of his hands, so that his flocks and herds are spread throughout the land. But stretch out your hand and strike everything he has, and he will surely curse you to your face."

The Lord said to Satan, "Very well, then, everything he has is in your power, but on the man himself do not lay a finger."

Then Satan went out from the presence of the Lord. (Job 1:6-12)

4. Why did God allow Satan to attack Job?

5. How did Satan attack Job?

• Job 1:13-19

• Job 2:7

One day when Job's sons and daughters were feasting and drinking wine at the oldest brother's house, a messenger came to Job and said, "The oxen were plowing and the donkeys were grazing nearby, and the Sabeans attacked and made off with them. They put the servants to the sword, and I am the only one who has escaped to tell you!"

While he was still speaking, another messenger came and said, "The fire of God fell from the sky and burned up the sheep and the servants, and I am the only one who has escaped to tell you!"

While he was still speaking, another messenger came and said, "The Chaldeans formed three raiding parties and swept down on your camels and made off with them. They put the servants to the sword, and I am the only one who has escaped to tell you!"

While he was still speaking, yet another messenger came and said, "Your sons and daughters were feasting and drinking wine at the oldest brother's house, when suddenly a mighty wind swept in from the desert and struck the four corners of the house. It collapsed on them and they are dead, and I am the only one who has escaped to tell you!" (Job 1:13-19)

So Satan went out from the presence of the Lord and afflicted Job with painful sores from the soles of his feet to the crown of his head. (Job 2:7)

6. Have you sensed that Satan has attacked you or your family lately? If so, how?

7. How did you respond to this attack?

8. Why do you think God would allow Satan to attack you?

Tomorrow we'll continue to apply Job's life to our own. Today, let's close in prayer and thank God for the example of Job.

Dear God,

Thank you for Job's life, and the example he is to my life. Thank you for being present in my life even when I'm going through trials. Give me the courage and strength to remain faithful when life gets messy. Amen.

DAY 2—A BUMP IN THE ROAD (CONTINUED)

Yesterday we began reading the story of Job, a man who was faithful to and blessed by God. We also read how Satan attacked Job and took away his children, his possessions, and his health. Today we'll look at the responses of Job's friends and family, and Job's response to God. We'll then apply Job's example to our own lives.

Reread Job 2 and answer the questions.

1. How does Job's wife respond to these trials? (Job 2:9)

His wife said to him, "Are you still maintaining your integrity? Curse God and die!" (Job 2:9)

2. How does Job respond to his wife? (Job 2:10)

He replied, "You are talking like a foolish woman. Shall we accept good from God, and not trouble?" In all this, Job did not sin in what he said. (Job 2:10)

3. Which response do you identify with more? Explain.

4. Read Job 38–41 then briefly summarize God's explanation for why he allowed Job to suffer these trials.

Job 38

Then the Lord spoke to Job out of the storm. He said:

"Who is this that obscures my plans with words without knowledge?

Prepare to defend yourself; I will question you, and you shall answer me.

"Where were you when I laid the earth's foundation? Tell me, if you understand.

Who marked off its dimensions? Surely you know! Who stretched a measuring line across it?

On what were its footings set, or who laid its cornerstone—while the morning stars sang together and all the angels shouted for joy?

Who shut up the sea behind doors when it burst forth from the womb,

when I made the clouds its garment and wrapped it in thick darkness,

when I fixed limits for it and set its doors and bars in place,

when I said, 'This far you may come and no farther; here is where your proud waves halt'?

"Have you ever given orders to the morning, or shown the dawn its place,
that it might take the earth by the edges and shake the wicked out of it?

The earth takes shape like clay under a seal; its features stand out like those of a garment.

The wicked are denied their light, and their upraised arm is broken.

"Have you journeyed to the springs of the sea or walked in the recesses of the deep?

Have the gates of death been shown to you? Have you seen the gates of the deepest darkness?

Have you comprehended the vast expanses of the earth? Tell me, if you know all this.

"What is the way to the abode of light? And where does darkness reside?

Can you take them to their places? Do you know the paths to their dwellings?

Surely you know, for you were already born! You have lived so many years!

"Have you entered the storehouses of the snow or seen the storehouses of the hail, which I reserve for times of trouble, for days of war and battle?

What is the way to the place where the lightning is dispersed, or the place where the east winds are scattered over the earth?

Who cuts a channel for the torrents of rain, and a path for the thunderstorm,

to water a land where no one lives, an uninhabited desert,

to satisfy a desolate wasteland and make it sprout with grass?

Does the rain have a father? Who fathers the drops of dew?

From whose womb comes the ice? Who gives birth to the frost from the heavens

when the waters become hard as stone, when the surface of the deep is frozen?

"Can you bind the chains of the Pleiades? Can you loosen Orion's belt?

Can you bring forth the constellations in their seasons or lead out the Bear with its cubs?

Do you know the laws of the heavens? Can you set up [God's] dominion over the earth?

"Can you raise your voice to the clouds and cover yourself with a flood of water?

Do you send the lightning bolts on their way? Do they report to you, 'Here we are'?

Who gives the ibis wisdom [about the flooding of the Nile], or gives the rooster understanding [of when to crow]?

Who has the wisdom to count the clouds? Who can tip over the water jars of the heavens

when the dust becomes hard and the clods of earth stick together?

"Do you hunt the prey for the lioness and satisfy the hunger of the lions

when they crouch in their dens or lie in wait in a thicket?

Who provides food for the raven when its young cry out to God and wander about for lack of food?

Job 39

"Do you know when the mountain goats give birth? Do you watch when the doe bears her fawn?

Do you count the months till they bear? Do you know the time they give birth?

They crouch down and bring forth their young; their labor pains are ended.

Their young thrive and grow strong in the wilds; they leave and do not return. "Who let the wild donkey go free? Who untied its ropes?

I gave it the wasteland as its home, the salt flats as its habitat.

It laughs at the commotion in the town; it does not hear a driver's shout.

It ranges the hills for its pasture and searches for any green thing.

"Will the wild ox consent to serve you? Will it stay by your manger at night?

Can you hold it to the furrow with a harness? Will it till the valleys behind you?

Will you rely on it for its great strength? Will you leave your heavy work to it?

Can you trust it to haul in your grain and bring it to your threshing floor?

"The wings of the ostrich flap joyfully, though they cannot compare with the wings and feathers of the stork.

She lays her eggs on the ground and lets them warm in the sand, unmindful that a foot may crush them, that some wild animal may trample them.

She treats her young harshly, as if they were not hers; she cares not that her labor was in vain,

for God did not endow her with wisdom or give her a share of good sense.

Yet when she spreads her feathers to run, she laughs at horse and rider.

"Do you give the horse its strength or clothe its neck with a flowing mane?

Do you make it leap like a locust, striking terror with its proud snorting?

It paws fiercely, rejoicing in its strength, and charges into the fray.

It laughs at fear, afraid of nothing; it does not shy away from the sword.

The quiver rattles against its side, along with the flashing spear and lance.

In frenzied excitement it eats up the ground; it cannot stand still when the trumpet sounds.

At the blast of the trumpet it snorts, 'Aha!' It catches the scent of battle from afar, the shout of commanders and the battle cry.

"Does the hawk take flight by your wisdom and spread its wings toward the south?

Does the eagle soar at your command and build its nest on high?

It dwells on a cliff and stays there at night; a rocky crag is its stronghold.

From there it looks for food; its eyes detect it from afar.

Its young ones feast on blood, and where the slain are, there it is."

Job 40
The Lord said to Job:

"Will the one who contends with the Almighty correct him? Let him who accuses God answer him!"

Then Job answered the Lord:

I am unworthy—how can I reply to you? I put my hand over my mouth.

I spoke once, but I have no answer—twice, but I will say no more."

Then the Lord spoke to Job out of the storm:

"Prepare to defend yourself; I will question you, and you shall answer me.

"Would you discredit my justice? Would you condemn me to justify yourself?

Do you have an arm like God's, and can your voice thunder like his?

Then adorn yourself with glory and splendor, and clothe yourself in honor and majesty.

Unleash the fury of your wrath, look at all who are proud and bring them low,

look at all who are proud and humble them, crush the wicked where they stand.

Bury them all in the dust together; shroud their faces in the grave.

Then I myself will admit to you that your own right hand can save you.

"Look at the behemoth, which I made along with you and which feeds on grass like an ox.

What strength it has in its loins, what power in the muscles of its belly!

Its tail sways like a cedar; the sinews of its thighs are close-knit.

Its bones are tubes of bronze, its limbs like rods of iron.

It ranks first among the works of God, yet its Maker can approach it with his sword.

The hills bring it their produce, and all the wild animals play nearby.

Under the lotus plants it lies, hidden among the reeds in the marsh.

The lotuses conceal it in their shadow; the poplars by the stream surround it.

A raging river does not alarm it; it is secure, though the Jordan should surge against its mouth.

Can anyone capture it by the eyes, or trap it and pierce its nose?

Job 41

"Can you pull in the leviathan with a fishhook or tie down its tongue with a rope?

Can you put a cord through its nose or pierce its jaw with a hook?

Will it keep begging you for mercy? Will it speak to you with gentle words?

Will it make an agreement with you for you to take it as your slave for life?

Can you make a pet of it like a bird or put it on a leash for the young women in your house?

Will traders barter for it? Will they divide it up among the merchants?

Can you fill its hide with harpoons or its head with fishing spears?

If you lay a hand on it, you will remember the struggle and never do it again!

Any hope of subduing it is false; the mere sight of it is overpowering.

No one is fierce enough to rouse it. Who then is able to stand against me?

Who has a claim against me that I must pay? Everything under heaven belongs to me.

"I will not fail to speak of Leviathan's limbs, its strength and its graceful form.

Who can strip off its outer coat? Who can penetrate its double coat of armor?

Who dares open the doors of its mouth, ringed about with fearsome teeth?

Its back has rows of shields tightly sealed together;

each is so close to the next that no air can pass between.

They are joined fast to one another; they cling together and cannot be parted.

Its snorting throws out flashes of light; its eyes are like the rays of dawn.

Flames stream from its mouth; sparks of fire shoot out.

Smoke pours from its nostrils as from a boiling pot over burning reeds.

Its breath sets coals ablaze, and flames dart from its mouth.

Strength resides in its neck; dismay goes before it.

The folds of its flesh are tightly joined; they are firm and immovable.

Its chest is hard as rock, hard as a lower millstone.

When it rises up, the mighty are terrified; they retreat before its thrashing.

The sword that reaches it has no effect, nor does the spear or the dart or the javelin.

Iron it treats like straw and bronze like rotten wood.

Arrows do not make it flee; slingstones are like chaff to it.

A club seems to it but a piece of straw; it laughs at the rattling of the lance.

Its undersides are jagged potsherds, leaving a trail in the mud like a threshing sledge.

It makes the depths churn like a boiling caldron and stirs up the sea like a pot of ointment.

It leaves a glistening wake behind it; one would think the deep had white hair.

Nothing on earth is its equal—a creature without fear.

It looks down on all that are haughty; it is king over all that are proud."

5. Within these four chapters in the book of Job, which chapters/passages/verses mean the most to you? How will you apply them to your life?

6. In your own words, summarize what God teaches us through the book of Job.

7. How does this apply to the trials you experience, including your parents' divorce?

Close your time with the following prayer: "Dear God, help me respond to the trials in my life the way Job responded. I pray I would trust in your love and your plan for me. Help me to cling to my faith in times of trouble, knowing you are with me. Amen."

DAY 3—BLESSED BE YOUR NAME

We spent the past two days gleaning truths and lessons from Job's life. Today we'll explore a popular Christian song called "Blessed Be Your Name" written by Matt Redman and Beth Redman and performed by Tree63. We'll analyze the lyrics and apply them to Job's life and our own.

Before we begin, read over the lyrics of the song at least twice. I also encourage you to listen to the song if you own Tree63's CD *The Answer to the Question* (Inpop Records, 2004). Or you can download the song from iTunes.

"Blessed Be Your Name"

Blessed be Your name
In the land that is plentiful
Where Your streams of abundance flow
Blessed be Your name

Blessed be Your name
When I'm found in the desert place
Though I walk through the wilderness
Blessed be Your name

Every blessing You pour out
I'll turn back to praise
When the darkness closes in, Lord
Still I will say

Blessed be the name of the Lord
Blessed be Your name
Blessed be the name of the Lord
Blessed be Your glorious name

Blessed be Your name
When the sun's shining down on me
When the world's 'all as it should be'
Blessed be Your name

Blessed be Your name
On the road marked with suffering
Though there's pain in the offering
Blessed be Your name

Every blessing you pour out
I'll turn back to praise
When the darkness closes in, Lord
Still I will say

Blessed be the name of the Lord
Blessed be Your name
Blessed be the name of the Lord
Blessed be Your glorious name

Blessed be the name of the Lord
Blessed be Your name
Blessed be the name of the Lord
Blessed be Your glorious name

You give and take away
You give and take away
My heart will choose to say
Lord, blessed be Your name

1. What's your initial reaction to this song?

The singer proclaims he will praise God "in the land that is plentiful, where Your streams of abundance flow."

2. Describe how Job's "land was plentiful."

3. How is your "land plentiful"?

Praising God is easy when God blesses us with a loving family, loyal friends, a nice house, plenty of food, a spot on the varsity track team, a new car, the hottest video game system, and trendy clothes.

But what's our response when we find ourselves driving down "the road marked with suffering"? Tree63 says they will praise God.

4. We already explored Job's suffering earlier this week. Now take a moment to describe your personal "road marked with suffering."

5. How did you respond to God during this time of trial? Check all that apply:

❏ I became angry with God.
❏ I yelled at God.
❏ I questioned God's existence.
❏ I questioned God's love for me.
❏ I ignored God; I stopped praying and reading my Bible.
❏ I thanked God for the blessings he's given to me.
❏ I praised God.

6. In your own words, describe what the singer means when he says, "though there's pain in the offering, blessed be Your name."

The singer acknowledges that when we experience trials, it's emotionally and spiritually difficult for us to praise God. Our sinful nature discourages us from praising God and encourages us to blame God. Praising God during difficult circumstances is painful for us, yet God wants us to do it anyway.

In order to praise God throughout your trials, you must first possess a humble heart.

You must acknowledge that God—not you—is in control. You must admit you see things through limited vision, but God sees things through his all-knowing lens.

7. Describe a time when you praised God during a difficult time in your life. If you cannot recall a time like this, then pray that God would give you the faith you need to praise him during difficult times.

8. Describe your reaction to the lyrics, "You give and take away, You give and take away, My heart will choose to say, Lord blessed be Your name"?

To be honest, I initially reacted to these lyrics with anger. How can I praise a God who gives and takes away at his leisure, with no regard for what I want? But then I realized that I bathed my response with pride, a sense of entitlement, and a weak faith. I must learn to trust that if God takes something away from my life (a person, a position, an opportunity), it's according to God's plan and good purpose.

God promises that "in all things God works for the good of those who love him" (Romans 8:28). God doesn't promise all things are good things. Cancer isn't good. Drunk driving isn't good. Divorce isn't good. God does promise, however, he will pour his love and blessings on us through all things if we're seeking his will. God wants only the best for his children.

Take some time now to praise God, even if your parents' divorce has been especially difficult for you lately…even if you feel lonely…even if you're unsure about the future…even if you're angry. Praise God. Write your words of praise here.

DAY 4—AM I DOOMED?

Browsing through a quaint gift shop, I stumbled upon a pillow with these words monogrammed on it: "Mirror, mirror on the wall, I am my mother after all." Really? Is this true? Many children try to avoid becoming like their parents, only to realize one day that they've become their parents.

But does this mean we're doomed to divorce as well? If we pick up our parents' mannerisms and beliefs, won't we also repeat their mistakes? Not necessarily. Let's discuss how we can avoid the pain of divorce in our own marriages.

First, you must understand who you are in Christ. We often hear people who are looking for a way out of their marriage say, "I'm not the same person I was when we married…I've changed…My needs have changed." But many people don't understand their identity in Christ, and this lack of understanding affects their marriage.

1. If you asked your friends to describe you, what would they say? Athletic? Smart? Beautiful? Take a moment to list all the qualities and characteristics that describe you.

- Strengths:

- Weaknesses:

- Gifts/Talents:

Now let's take a moment to think about who you are in Christ. First Samuel 16:7 says, "Do not consider his appearance or his height…The Lord does not look at the things human beings look at. People look at the outward appearance, but the Lord looks at the heart."

Your identity in Christ is simple: You are God's child. God loves you simply because he created you. And God created you to glorify him on this earth.

Read Psalm 139:13-16 and answer the questions below.

For you created my inmost being; you knit me together in my mother's womb.

I praise you because I am fearfully and wonderfully made; your works are wonderful, I know that full well.

My frame was not hidden from you when I was made in the secret place. When I was woven together in the depths of the earth,

your eyes saw my unformed body. All the days ordained for me were written in your book before one of them came to be. (Psalm 139:13-16)

2. Who created you?

3. What does the psalmist mean when he says he is "fearfully and wonderfully made"?

According to verses 15-16, God knew you and your unique personhood before he even created you. That's tough to wrap our brains around, but it's also amazing! God knows every intimate detail about you, and God has known these things since before you even physically existed.

Psalm 139 shows how much care God took in creating you. Earlier you listed some attributes that describe your unique personality. So how can you use this knowledge to glorify God?

First, know God created you purposefully. God has a unique mission for each of us.

Next, consider how you can use your gifts to get involved in God's mission for your life. If you listed leadership as one of your qualities, God can use you to get others involved in ministry projects. Are you kind and compassionate? God can use you to minister to hurting people. Do you play the guitar or sing? God can use your musical gifts to help others engage in worship.

"Great, but how does this help me in marriage?" you might ask.

Well, you must first understand your strengths, weaknesses, and talents so you know what God wants you to do in life. If you want to pursue a career that involves travel, then you probably shouldn't marry someone who's a homebody. Do you want to minister to underprivileged children? Then the person you marry should share your desire. This doesn't mean your spouse must serve in the trenches with you, but he or she must support the time and effort you invest in other people.

Learning your identity in Christ takes time. Start by exploring your characteristics and interests. Then pray and ask God to show you how he wants you to use the gifts he's given you. God will undoubtedly reveal his plans for you in his time.

Second, as we learn who we are as individuals, we must also try to understand why our parents divorced. (We discussed the importance of this in Week Two's lesson.) When you know why your parents divorced, you can avoid those same mistakes.

For instance, money is one of the main issues that leads to divorce in marriages today. If your parents constantly fought about money, then you can make financial responsibility a priority in your life—starting today. You can learn how to budget your money, how to stay out of debt, and how to honor God with money through giving, spending, and saving. Whatever the problem was in their marriage, take time to explore your parents' mistakes in this area, and how you can protect yourself against making those same mistakes.

Third, we must take responsibility for our own choices. In the book of Ezekiel, God says we're each responsible for our own sins.

4. Read Ezekiel 18:19-20 and summarize the verses in the space provided.

"Yet you ask, 'Why does the son not share the guilt of his father?' Since the son has done what is just and right and has been careful to keep all my decrees, he will surely live. The one who sins is the one who will die. The child will not share the guilt of the parent, nor will the parent share the guilt of the child. The righteousness of the righteous will be credited to them, and the wickedness of the wicked will be charged against them." (Ezekiel 18:19-20)

God clearly points out that we won't be punished for someone else's sin. If our parents sin, God will deal with them. However, we still have the opportunity to choose obedience in Christ.

5. How do these verses apply to divorce in your life?

Finally, we can avoid the pain of divorce by seeking God daily. Many people divorce because they allow other things in their lives to take priority over their relationship with God. Work, sports, extracurricular activities—all these things consume our time. God wants you to make time with him a priority. Being in community with God and living in his will is the most perfect place for us. Practicing the discipline of a daily quiet time and prayer time now will prepare you for the joys and trials you'll face in the future.

Comedian and actor Jim Carrey remarked about his relationship with actress Jenny McCarthy, "We're never getting married, but we're never getting divorced."[24] While Carrey might avoid the difficulties of marriage, he also misses out on the blessings that God's plan for marriage brings. I hope you don't adopt this same negative attitude toward marriage.

After working through today's lesson, I hope you agree that you're not doomed. Satan would love for you to believe you're damaged goods, unworthy of love, and destined to divorce. But these are Satan's lies. God's truth tells us you're God's precious creation, worthy of receiving and giving love, and destined to make your own God-honoring choices in life.

Take the time now to pray and ask God to reveal your unique talents and gifts and how you can use those to honor him. Write down this prayer.

DAY 5—GROWING CLOSER TO CHRIST THROUGH DIVORCE

You made it! You've finished this study! You've bravely traveled through many areas of your life to gain a new perspective on your parents' divorce. Throughout your journey you've probably experienced bumpy roads, unfamiliar terrain, dangerous intersections, cautious turns, and confusing signs. But I hope you've stuck with the study, pressed on through the more difficult lessons, and truly reflected on God's love and purpose for you as a result of your parents' divorce.

Today we want to look at one last passage that relates to life after our parents' divorce.

1. Read Jeremiah 6:16 and summarize it in your own words.

This is what the Lord says: "Stand at the crossroads and look; ask for the ancient paths, ask where the good way is, and walk in it, and you will find rest for your souls." (Jeremiah 6:16)

Several times throughout this study we've discussed standing at a crossroads. When you face any trial in your life, you'll eventually reach a crossroads: A time when you must choose a path. Choose left and you'll face destruction, heartache, and disappointment. Choose right and you'll experience love, joy, and peace.

In this verse God told his people to "stand at the crossroads and *look*." God didn't create us to be mindless robots. God wants his children to weigh their options. God wants us to look at the left and the right paths and evaluate the choices and consequences of both.

2. Then God tells us to "ask." What does God want us to ask for?

Ancient paths are God's timeless commands and truths for living a righteous life. And these paths have been tested throughout history. God wants us to choose the right path—not because he tells us to do so, but because the right path has proven itself worthy in the lives of the many people who've lived before us. God doesn't want us to experience pain. Instead he wants us to learn from the pain and mistakes of others so we can choose a better way to live.

3. After we "look" and "ask," what's God's next command for us?

God tells us to evaluate our options ("look"), learn from past mistakes ("ask"), and then choose the right path ("walk in it"). Think about this for minute. Let's pretend you want to go hiking. You ask an experienced hiker, who has hiked every trail on the mountain, which trails you should avoid and which you should follow. He draws a map for you and highlights the dangerous, life-threatening path you should avoid. He also points out the challenging, yet rewarding path that will improve your hiking skills and give you an enjoyable hiking experience. Which path would you choose?

Hopefully, if you trust the experienced hiker, you choose the challenging, yet rewarding path. This isn't taking the easy way out. Choosing the right path is the wiser, more mature decision because you know it protects you from unnecessary danger.

4. If we "look," "ask," and "walk," what does God promise us as his children?

God promises us we'll find rest. We'll experience overwhelming peace, joy, and contentment—even in the bumpy, rough parts of the trail. Unfortunately, your parents' divorce isn't the last difficult road you'll travel in life. Life brings sickness, death, job loss, and other disappointments and tragedies.

I'm not trying to deliver a message of doom and gloom, but I do want you to realize the skills you've learned over the past five weeks—forgiveness, communication, working through your emotions—will help you persevere through many other trials in life. And not only persevere, but ultimately grow closer to Christ.

The apostle Paul promises that "suffering produces perseverance; perseverance, character; and character, hope" (Romans 5:3-4). We can use the trials of life to develop a persevering spirit. This determination will develop our character and lead to hope—a hope in a new life through Jesus Christ.

As we finish our time together, take a moment to ask yourself the following questions.

5. Am I standing at a crossroads in my walk with Christ?

6. Do I see a path to the left paved with doubt, frustration, anger, and rebellion? Explain.

7. Do I see a path to the right paved with forgiveness, love, peace, and joy? Explain.

8. Have I sought God's forgiveness and grace in my life by accepting Christ as my Savior? If so, how has that changed my life? If not, will I accept God's calling today?

As a child of divorce, I've experienced similar thoughts and emotions to the ones you've probably experienced as a result of your parents' divorce. Though I wish I could, I cannot sit with you and comfort you.

The good news is Jesus Christ also knows your every thought and emotion. Psalm 139:1-3 tells us, "You have searched me, Lord, and you know me. You know when I sit and when I rise; you perceive my thoughts from afar. You discern my going out and my lying down; you are familiar with all my ways."

Jesus is ready and willing to sit with you in your time of need. Won't you sit at Jesus' feet and allow him to usher in his healing and blessings?

Thank you for embarking on this journey with me. I know it's been a difficult road. I pray this study has equipped you so whenever you stand at a crossroads, you'll choose Christ!

GROUP SESSION
WEEK SIX—THE END OF THE ROAD
Growing Closer to Christ

GOAL

This week we'll try to understand God's role in suffering and trials and apply these truths to our own lives in order to grow closer to Christ.

SUGGESTED ICEBREAKER

Let the students listen to "Blessed Be Your Name" performed by Tree63 (*The Answer to the Question*, 2004). The lyrics are printed in Week Six, Day Three of the Student Guide. You might suggest they read the words of the song as they listen to the music.

After the song ends, discuss the following questions:

1. What's the singer's response to the blessings in his life?

2. What's the singer's response to the trials in his life?

3. Explain why it's difficult to praise God when he "takes away."

4. How do you feel about the statement: "You give and take away"? Does God have the right to do this?

5. What's the main message of the song?

6. How does this song apply to your life in light of your parents' divorce?

7. How can you grow closer to God through the trial of divorce?

GROUP DISCUSSION

This past week the students read passages from the book of Job. Review Job's life and engage the students in a group discussion using the following questions.

1. What kind of a man was Job? (Job 1:1-5)

In the land of Uz there lived a man whose name was Job. This man was blameless and upright; he feared God and shunned evil. He had seven sons and three daughters, and he owned seven thousand sheep, three thousand camels, five hundred yoke of oxen and five hundred donkeys, and had a large number of servants. He was the greatest man among all the people of the East.

His sons used to take turns holding feasts in their homes, and they would invite their three sisters to eat and drink with them. When a period of feasting had run its course, Job would make arrangements for them to be purified. Early in the morning he would sacrifice a burnt offering for each of them, thinking, "Perhaps my children have sinned and cursed God in their hearts." This was Job's regular custom. (Job 1:1-5)

- Faithful
- Blessed with relationships and material/financial possessions
- Generous
- Concerned about his children's spiritual lives

2. Why did Satan want to attack Job? (Job 1:8-11)

Then the Lord said to Satan, "Have you considered my servant Job? There is no one on earth like him; he is blameless and upright, a man who fears God and shuns evil."

"Does Job fear God for nothing?" Satan replied. "Have you not put a hedge around him and his household and everything he has? You have blessed the work of his hands, so that his flocks and herds are spread throughout the land. But stretch out your hand and strike everything he has, and he will surely curse you to your face." (Job 1:8-11)

- Because Job was blessed, and it's easy to be faithful to God when there are no trials in life.
- He wanted to prove that people's faith is fleeting.

3. Why did God allow Satan to attack Job? (Job 38–41)

- It provides insight into the issue of suffering.
- It gives an explanation of why good people suffer.
- It shows that God's relationship with us relies on grace (not retribution).
- It shows that we cannot earn God's blessings through good works. God has control over whom he blesses.
- It shows that we cannot secure God's blessings by being obedient.

If your group meets for 12 weeks, wrap up the session after discussing the story of Job and close simply in prayer and be open to any questions from your students. When you meet again in Week 12, review this book and then engage the students in a group discussion using the questions below. These questions will help the students apply the principles they learned from Job's life to their own lives.

As an icebreaker for Week 12, ask how they're feeling this week in general. Has anything happened in the past week that has stirred up strong emotions? Use this as a time to allow students to open up, encourage one another, and move to a deeper, more personal level of sharing.

You may also wish to use the Closing Activity listed here as the Closing Activity for Week 12.

Remind your students to read over their Week 11 (Chapter Six) homework on growing closer to Jesus before you meet again.

4. Do you ever feel like Job? Why or why not?

5. How has Satan attacked your life? Your family?

6. How have you responded to Satan's attacks?

7. Do you believe God wants the best for you? Explain.

8. Do you think God is punishing you through your parents' divorce? Explain.

9. How should you respond to the trials in your life?

CLOSING ACTIVITY

Let the students listen to "When Love Takes You In" by Steven Curtis Chapman (*Declaration*, 2001; or *All About Love*, 2003). You might want to find the lyrics online and print copies of them so the students can read the words of the song while they listen.

After the song ends, discuss the following questions:

1. This song explores the feelings of loneliness and isolation. Have you experienced these feelings as a result of your parents divorce? If so, explain.

2. How can Christ's love change your life?

3. When parents divorce, it's easy to be angry with them and with God. It's easy to turn away from God. How has this Bible study helped you turn toward God instead of away from him?

SIGN-IN SHEET

NAME	PHONE	EMAIL	GRADE

SAMPLE LETTER TO PARENTS

Dear Parents,

We want to let you know about an exciting new program we're starting at (church name). The program is called *Dealing with Divorce*. This (six-week or 12-week) study will help your teenager work through the questions, emotions, and thoughts that surround divorce.

Each student will receive a Student Guide that contains six weekly Bible studies covering the following topics:

- Feelings about divorce
- Reasons why parents divorce
- Changes families experience after divorce
- How to effectively communicate with parents
- Forgiveness
- How they can grow closer to Christ through trials such as divorce

We encourage you to attend a parent information meeting on _____. We look forward to this time to take a closer look at this program with you and answer any questions you might have.

Then during the weekly Group Sessions, we'll dive deeper into each of these topics through group discussions and activities. Both the Student and Leader's Guides were written by Elizabeth Oates and published by Youth Specialties/Zondervan.

If you have any questions you'd like to ask outside of the information meeting, please feel free to contact (name of youth worker or person in charge of this program).

We believe this ministry will meet the needs of our students, and we ask for your prayers as we prepare to minister to many hurting students who are struggling with their parents' divorce.

Sincerely,

(Church staff member's name)
(Church name)

SUGGESTED READING LIST FOR STUDENTS

Abbas, Jen. *Generation Ex: Adult Children of Divorce and the Healing of Our Pain.* Colorado Springs: Waterbrook Press, 2004.

DiMarco, Hayley. *Stupid Parents: Why They Just Don't Understand and How You Can Help.* New York: Fleming H. Revell, 2006.

SUGGESTED READING LIST FOR PARENTS

The following is a list of books that offer insight into the struggles that children of divorce face both immediately after the divorce and years later. These books will help parents understand the emotions their children experience but are often unable to express.

Abbas, Jen. *Generation Ex: Adult Children of Divorce and the Healing of Our Pain.* Colorado Springs: Waterbrook Press, 2004.

Aldrich, Sandra P. *From One Single Mother to Another: Heart-Lifting Encouragement and Practical Advice.* Ventura, Calif.: Regal Books, Revised Edition 2005.

Coleman, William L. *What Children Need to Know When Parents Get Divorced.* Bloomington, Minn.: Bethany House, 1998.

Hart, Dr. Archibald. *Helping Children Survive Divorce: What to Expect; How to Help.* Nashville: Thomas Nelson, Revised and Updated Edition 1997.

Klumpp, Mike. *The Single Dad's Survival Guide: How to Succeed as a One-Man Parenting Team.* Colorado Springs: Waterbrook Press, 2003.

Leman, Dr. Kevin. *Single Parenting That Works: Six Keys to Raising Happy, Healthy Children in a Single-Parent Home.* Carol Stream, Ill.: Tyndale House, 2006.

Wallerstein, Judith S., Julia M. Lewis, and Sandra Blakeslee. *The Unexpected Legacy of Divorce: The 25 Year Landmark Study.* New York: Hyperion, 2000.

NOTES

[1]Powerhouse Ministry, "Depression and Teens," battlecry.com, http://powerhouse-ministry.org/battle-cry_depression.aspx (accessed August 1, 2008).

[2]List adapted from Powerhouse Ministry, "Depression and Teens," battlecry.com, http://powerhouse-ministry.org/battlecry_depression.aspx, and National Institute of Mental Health (NIMH), "What are the symptoms of depression?" Depression booklet (Washington DC: U.S. Dept. of Health and Human Services, 2007), http://www.nimh.nih.gov/health/publications/depression/nimhdepression.pdf (accessed August 1, 2008).

[3]Judy Shepps Battle, "Teenagers and Suicide," About Teen Depression Web site (2002), http://www.about-teen-depression.com/teen-suicide.html (accessed August 1, 2008).

[4]"The Pursuit of Happyness," *The Oprah Winfrey Show*, (first aired November 22, 2006), "Homeless to Hollywood: Will Smith and the Real Chris Gardner," http://www.oprah.com/dated/oprahshow/oprahshow_20061122 (accessed August 1, 2008).

[5]Pat Davies, Melinda Smith, Tina de Benedictis, Jaelline Jaffe, and Jeanne Segal, "Domestic Violence and Abuse: Warning Signs and Symptoms of Abusive Relationships," helpguide.org (updated August 20, 2007), http://www.helpguide.org/mental/domestic_violence_abuse_types_signs_causes_effects.htm (accessed August 2, 2008).

[6]Ibid.

[7]"Abandonment," Miriam-Webster Online, http://www.m-w.com/dictionary/abandonment (accessed August 2, 2008).

[8]Jim Denison, "Hope for the Hurting Hearts," page 3—"What Constitutes a Biblical Divorce?" GodIssues.org, (January 12, 2003), http://www.godissues.org/articles/articles/178/3/Hope-For-The-Hurting-Hearts (accessed August 2, 2008).

[9]National Association for Children of Alcoholics (www.nacoa.org) as quoted in Hayley DiMarco, *Stupid Parents: Why They Just Don't Understand and How You Can Help* (Grand Rapids, Mich.: Fleming H. Revell , 2006), 121.

[10]Kimberly Read and Marcia Purse, "Addiction," Bipolar Disorder page of About.com: Health (September 25, 2006). http://bipolar.about.com/od/glossary/g/gl_addiction.htm?terms=definition+of%20 `ddiction (accessed August 2, 2008).

[11]All of the stories in this section are fictitious. They represent situations that actually occur in families, but they don't represent specific people.

[12]Philip Yancey, *Finding God in Unexpected Places* (New York: Doubleday, 2005), 15, as quoted, in part, in James A. Fowler, "Addiction," Commentaries and Study Outlines, Christ In You Ministries (1999), http://www.christinyou.net/pages/addiction.html (accessed August 2, 2008).

[13]Dr. Thomas L. Constable, "IV. Exhortations to Practical Christian Living 3:1–4:6," Notes on Colossians 2007 Edition, 39, soniclight.com, http://www.soniclight.com/constable/notes/pdf/colossians.pdf (accessed August 2, 2008).

[14]Ibid.

[15]Gary L. Thomas, *Sacred Marriage* (Grand Rapids, Mich.: Zondervan, 2000), 3.

[16]Dr. Thomas L. Constable, "IV. Moses' Second Major Address: An Exposition of the Law Chapters 5–26," Notes on Deuteronomy 2005 Edition, 82, soniclight.com http://www.soniclight.com/constable/notes/pdf/deuteronomy.pdf (accessed August 2, 2008).

[17]Ibid.

[18]AP Article, "Report: Obesity Will Reverse Life Expectancy Gains," Health, CNN.com (March 16, 2005), http://www.cnn.com/2005/HEALTH/diet.fitness/03/16/obesity.longevity.ap/index.html (accessed August 2, 2008).

[19]Dr. Thomas L. Constable, "V. Jesus' Ministry on the Way to Jerusalem 9:51–19:27," Notes on Luke 2008 Edition, 151, soniclight.com, http://www.soniclight.com/constable/notes/pdf/luke.pdf (accessed August 2, 2008).

[20]Judith S. Wallerstein, Julia M. Lewis, and Sandra Blakeslee, *The Unexpected Legacy of Divorce: A 25 Year Landmark Study* (New York: Hyperion Books, 2000), 56.

[21]Hayley DiMarco, *Stupid Parents: Why They Just Don't Understand and How You Can Help* (Grand Rapids, Mich.: Fleming H. Revell, 2006), 64.

[22]*The Unexpected Legacy of Divorce*, 239.

[23]*Stupid Parents*, 140.

[24]Janice Min, "I'll Never Marry," *US Weekly*, Issue 634 (April 9, 2007): 12.

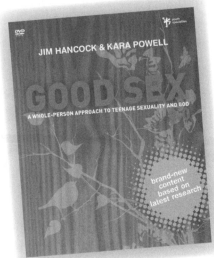

Today's teens live in a world saturated with sex, making it difficult for them to understand how their own sexuality fits into God's plan for their lives. Updated to include the latest in social science and sexual research among adolescents, *Good Sex 2.0* provides a DVD, 1 copy of the student journal, and 1 copy of the leader's guide—all the tools to help you (and parents of teens) involve your students in understanding, enjoying, and taking responsibility for their sexuality—all without lecturing, intimidating, or moralizing.

Good Sex 2.0
A Whole-Person Approach to Teenage Sexuality and God
Jim Hancock & Kara Powell
RETAIL $49.99
ISBN 978-0-310-28268-6

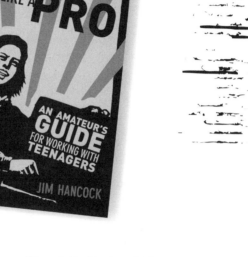

Being a volunteer youth worker can be exciting, intimidating, fulfilling, and challenging, and until now, there was no "manual" on how to be a volunteer in a youth ministry. *How to Volunteer Like a Pro* offers practical help and indispensable insights that will make your experience as a volunteer youth worker valuable and rewarding for you and your students.

How to Volunteer Like a Pro
An Amateur's Guide for Working with Teenagers
Jim Hancock
RETAIL $12.99
ISBN 978-0-310-28776-6

youth
specialties

In this DVD series from the Skit Guys, you'll find six weeks of everything you need to teach memorable lessons to your students on topics that really matter to them. Tommy and Eddie provide you with a Skit Guys video, a study guide, a message outline, and small group questions for six different lessons on each DVD—making it easier than ever for you to plan a lesson!

You Teach Volume 1
ISBN 978-0-310-28084-2

You Teach Volume 2
ISBN 978-0-310-28085-9

You Teach Volume 3
ISBN 978-0-310-28086-6

The Skit Guys
RETAIL $39.99